The Search for a Rela

In *The Search for a Relational Home*, Chris Jaenicke gives the reader an inside view of what actually happens in psychotherapy and how change occurs. He describes how both participants – the patient and the therapist – feel, and how they affect each other. The reader is encouraged to vicariously partake in the process from the perspective of his or her own life experiences.

The book describes the nature of therapeutic action through a radicalized version of intersubjective systems theory. It demonstrates how psychotherapy is an outcome of a highly personal encounter between two unique human beings, and how, while the goal of psychoanalysis is to help the patient, this can only be achieved inasmuch as both participants are willing to undergo transformation. Jaenicke clarifies how both successes and failures as well as personal strengths and weaknesses play a constitutive part in the psychotherapeutic process. *The Search for a Relational Home* also provides theoretical and practical guidelines for supervision.

Jaenicke presents here a unique approach to the process of psychotherapy which will be vital reading for psychoanalysts, psychotherapists and those in training as well as students in all fields of mental health.

Chris Jaenicke is a faculty member and training and supervising analyst at the Arbeitsgemeinschaft für Psychoanalyse und Psychotherapie, e.V. Berlin. He is in private practice in Berlin, Germany, and is the author of several previous books, including *Change in Psychoanalysis* (Routledge, 2011).

PSYCHOANALYTIC INQUIRY BOOK SERIES
JOSEPH D. LICHTENBERG
SERIES EDITOR

Like its counterpart, *Psychoanalytic Inquiry: A Topical Journal for Mental Health Professionals*, the Psychoanalytic Inquiry Book Series presents a diversity of subjects within a diversity of approaches to those subjects. Under the editorship of Joseph Lichtenberg, in collaboration with Melvin Bornstein and the editorial board of *Psychoanalytic Inquiry*, the volumes in this series strike a balance between research, theory, and clinical application. We are honored to have published the works of various innovators in psychoanalysis, such as Frank Lachmann, James Fosshage, Robert Stolorow, Donna Orange, Louis Sander, Léon Wurmser, James Grotstein, Joseph Jones, Doris Brothers, Fredric Busch, and Joseph Lichtenberg, among others.

The series includes books and monographs on mainline psychoanalytic topics, such as sexuality, narcissism, trauma, homosexuality, jealousy, envy, and varied aspects of analytic process and technique. In our efforts to broaden the field of analytic interest, the series has incorporated and embraced innovative discoveries in infant research, self-psychology, intersubjectivity, motivational systems, affects as process, responses to cancer, borderline states, contextualism, postmodernism, attachment research and theory, medication, and mentalization. As further investigations in psychoanalysis come to fruition, we seek to present them in readable, easily comprehensible writing.

After 25 years, the core vision of this series remains the investigation, analysis and discussion of developments at the cutting edge of the psychoanalytic field, inspired by a boundless spirit of inquiry.

PSYCHOANALYTIC INQUIRY BOOK SERIES
JOSEPH D. LICHTENBERG
SERIES EDITOR

PSYCHOANALYTIC INQUIRY BOOK SERIES
JOSEPH D. LICHTENBERG
SERIES EDITOR

PSYCHOANALYTIC INQUIRY BOOK SERIES
JOSEPH D. LICHTENBERG
SERIES EDITOR

The Search for
a Relational Home

An intersubjective view
of therapeutic action

Chris Jaenicke

Routledge
Taylor & Francis Group

LONDON AND NEW YORK

First published 2015
by Routledge
27 Church Road, Hove, East Sussex, BN3 2FA

and by Routledge
711 Third Avenue, New York, NY 10017

Routledge is an imprint of the Taylor & Francis Group, an informa business

British Library Cataloguing in Publication Data
A catalogue record for this book is available from the British Library

Library of Congress Cataloging in Publication Data
Jaenicke, Chris, 1946– author.
[Die Suche nach Bezogenheit. English]
  The search for a relational home : an intersubjective view of
  therapeutic action / Chris Jaenicke.
      p.; cm.
  Translation of: Die Suche nach Bezogenheit :
  Eine intersubjective Sicht therapeutischer Aktion /
  Chris Jaenicke, c2015.
  Includes bibliographical references and index.
  I. Title.
  [DNLM: 1. Psychotherapy. 2. Physician-Patient Relations.
  3. Psychoanalysis—methods. WM 420]
  RC480.5
  616.89'14—dc23   2014017022

ISBN: 978-1-138-79699-7 (hbk)
ISBN: 978-1-138-79700-0 (pbk)
ISBN: 978-1-315-75749-0 (ebk)

Typeset in Sabon
by RefineCatch Limited, Bungay, Suffolk

To my wife, Hilla Jaenicke

Contents

Acknowledgments

This book could not have been written without the helpful intersubjective fields that it was embedded in. Therefore, my thanks go to Routledge and my editors, Kate Hawes, Kirsten Buchanan, and Susannah Frearson who not only made the production possible, but who were also instrumental in making it a smooth process. I am grateful to those who read parts or all of my manuscript and gave me helpful feedback: Dorothee Adam-Lauterbach, Monika Amler, George Atwood, Andreas Bachhofen, Ruth Becker, Ronald Bodansky, Frank Horsetzky, Angelika Korp, Margit Murr, Lannie Peyton, Nicola Sahhar, Christine Schmidt, Christoph Seidler, Robert Stolorow, Jens Tiedemann, and Cordula Zimmermann. A special thanks also to Roger Frie, who edited a first, abbreviated version of Chapter 1 for the *International Journal of Psychoanalytic Self Psychology*, Volume 8, 3, 2013. I am grateful to H.-P. Königs who was supportive in the writing of this book. I want to thank George Atwood for his unrelenting belief in the dignity of suffering human beings and for providing the needed encouragement at pivotal moments in the writing process. Robert Stolorow has always been an inspiration in pursuing one's own authentic vision.

Chapter I

Basic premises

Thoughts on success, failure and cure in psychoanalysis

I'm yelling. I'm yelling as loud as I can, but no sound is coming out. I'm screaming, screaming so hard that the cords of my neck stand out. Even then only a barely audible croak comes out: "It's not the perfect cure that I want for my patients!" No answer from the person I'm addressing. In a final attempt to reach him I whisper: "You think what I'm doing is fascism?" The man raises his sharp chin and looks down at me out of the corner of his eagle-hooded eye, and says: "Yes, fascism."

This was a recent dream. In fact, it is a dream I have often in various scenarios, rageful screaming with no voice. George Atwood (2012) writes "Dreams are autobiographical microcosms, symbolizing the subjective life of the dreamer" (p. 90) According to Atwood (2012):

> Dreams capture something that is incomplete in one's conscious life. Impressions, feelings, memories, thoughts all in a swirl, not worked out, insufficiently articulated, incompletely thought through: This is the stuff of dreaming . . . and dreams are attempts to resolve subjective tensions.
>
> (p. 97)

One such tension in my dream is that I can't make myself heard. So why write another book? After the first two I always eagerly awaited reactions. When they came – and many were positive – they lifted me up. But it was like a brushfire feeling, quickly extinguished. This was when I understood, finally, that the holes I have within me won't be filled. I felt bereft, stripped, irrevocably flawed, but relieved. And yet, the question remains: What is cure? Are we cured, do we cure? After encounter groups, transactional analysis, Gestalt and body psychotherapy, a psychoanalytic training, a body psychotherapy training, and four analyses I am not cured. I'm better, I'm different. I've achieved some measure of professional expertise. I've overcome fears in the sense that now I know how afraid I've been. I still feel small. My strength is one which is compacted out of that which remains and part of that is my curiosity. The curiosity then is the leading edge of an inner tension, which finds some measure of temporary release in writing (Atwood, 2012). Creativity is one way out of simultaneous feelings of being and nothingness. What happens in psychotherapy and what, if anything, cures? How do we define success and failure? That's what this book is about. A continuation of my search. Answers? We will see. "It's only rock 'n' roll", the Rolling Stones sing; and, in my case: it is only psychoanalysis, but I like it.

We have come to understand that the therapeutic dyad is a system intertwined with and subject to the influence of a network of systems (Coburn, 2009; Boston Change Process Study Group, 2010). As part of a system, I argued in *Change in Psychoanalysis* (Jaenicke, 2011) that for a therapeutic process to succeed, both participants had to undergo change. In this book, I attempt to explain how it is our understanding of the patient–analyst dyad as a system that will further and deepen our understanding of how therapy works and how we can begin to conceptualize cure. Furthermore, it is my contention that in order to conceptualize the notion of cure, we must develop a new perspective on the notion of failure. I argue that failure and suffering are integral parts of our subjectivity, and that they serve as a valuable medium to allow us to learn how to be with one another. In-depth examinations of the interaction of differently organized subjective worlds in psychotherapy show how closely weakness and strength, cure and failure are entwined in any psychotherapeutic process. The negotiations of limitations and failures of both participants are pivotal for an understanding of the therapeutic treatments we engage in. Sometimes what we may consider to be our strengths will lead to failure, while our limitations may be considered as helpful. On the level of the bi-directional encounter, the process of cure has to do with how the idiosyncratic strengths and short-comings of both participants become entangled and are subsequently dealt with in the working-through process. While this provides the basis of our silent understanding of the therapeutic process, the asymmetric setting is upheld and the focus of our work remains on our patients.

In my previous work I have tried to show how interwoven our subjectivity is with our choice of theories and with our clinical practice. A related goal is to be able to do this in the *way* that I write.

Hence, I began this book with a dream that will serve as a frame for the questions that I will pursue. I hope to use my own subjectivity and the way I write about it, ". . . in a form to which others can relate in empathic dialogue" (Atwood and Stolorow, 1984, p. 7); a form of communication which includes dreams, associations, snippets of songs, metaphors, and personal meanings in order to better bridge the gulf between the idiosyncracy of my subjectivity and "the experience of being human in universal terms" (p. 7). In much the same manner, the intersubjective field, in which patients can come to their own truthfulness, is particularly well suited to demonstrate the potential of shared human possibilities.

If I interpret my dream as a part of my pathology I could understand the lack of my voice as a problem of self-definition and myself as an "as-if-personality". I could view my disorder as a "basic fault" whose developmental origins lie in a lack of primary love (Balint, 1968): my failure to find a voice for my fallibility and to be heard by my rejecting listener resulting in a failed attempt to be reconciled with my imperfection. What do the realization that I am not "cured" and the fear that I cannot cure then mean? Perhaps there is no cure? Are "the holes I have within me that can't be filled" my transience, my incompleteness, my death? I suspect that my dream about cure was a flawed attempt to free myself from the shackles of pathological accommodation (Brandchaft *et al.*, 2010), my soundless scream a sabotaged attempt at authenticity, a plea to be accepted, despite a felt demand for implacable perfection – an illusory attempt to gain a love that was long lost or never given?

If I follow my feelings about myself as failed and small further, I arrive at a core conviction that I am not here. I do not exist. That is the basis of my lack of voice and my deepest terror. In *The Abyss of Madness* (2012) Atwood describes states of annihilation as extreme forms of pathological accommodation. And yet, I am. I was helped, I do help. But in my heart of hearts, both states exist. All of these thoughts form the background; frame my questions concerning cure. What is the counter-part to my basic feelings of non-existence and terror? I suspect that I may have to re-define my understanding of cure. As Keith Richards says: "It's good to be here . . . it's good to be anywhere" (Scorsese, 2007).

When we speak of our patients we may say someone is in a state of fragmentation, dissociation, denial, or as feeling rejected, excluded or so alone as to feel bereft. Such states lend themselves and often are safely ensconced in the otherness known as patients, but therapists need not see themselves exempt from such feeling-states. Since my 20s, I have been afflicted from time to time, seemingly inexplicably, with a feeling of bleeding out internally. I feel extremely vulnerable then with a desire to vanish. I understand this as fantasy in which escape comes at the price of annihilation, in an imagined identification with those who didn't see me, a union in nothingness. Perhaps the antidote to the internal wound is not happiness, but a relational home for those of us whose despair takes the form of feeling invisible. The experience of exclusion and the concomitant feeling of "existential shame" (Jaenicke, 2011), both intricately linked with the experience of annihilation may be so profound that it is often not in reflective awareness, while at the same time being distributed in so many systems of relatedness as to centrally organize our experiential worlds. When, finally, within reflective reach, in the safety of an analyst-patient dyad, it may result in states of excruciating terror in our patients. He or she feels excluded or rejected doesn't cover it, doesn't begin to convey the feeling from within. This is why one of self-psychology's central contributions to psychoanalysis – namely, the need for deeply validating understanding, cannot be overemphasized.

If I reflect further on my own experiences of feelings of annihilation, I would go back to a dream that I had in my training analysis almost 30 years ago. In the dream my earlobe was pierced by a golden nail. The nail symbolized my feeling that I couldn't escape listening to the suffering of my mother. The theme of pathological accommodation is not new to the genesis of the making of an analyst. I mention it to underscore my point that for those of us in a profession dealing with suffering, our own suffering plays an intricate, ongoing and irrevocable part in each of our encounters with our patients. It is not our patients who are called upon to understand or be responsive to our pain, it is we ourselves. Shame, that ghostly jailor, prevents us from accepting this as a matter of course. In this context, which I have called the myth of the healthy healer, it is not so important *what* happened to me, but that I don't deny it. My friend Robert Stolorow (personal communication, 12 April 2012) referred to "the myth of the healthy healer" as an oxymoron.

In order to put what I have written about myself in a theoretical framework and to explain my objective, I again quote Atwood and Stolorow (1984) in full:

> Psychoanalytic histories must ... go beyond the narrative ... they must bridge the gulf between the concrete particularity of an

individual life and the experience of being human in universal terms. The task of writing a psychoanalytic narrative is one of transposing the analyst's understanding into a presentation illuminating the life under study for the intellectual community at large. This means unveiling the experiences of that life in a form to which others can relate their own personal worlds in empathic dialogue. The intersubjective field of the analysis serves a mediating function in this regard, providing the initial basis of comparison for describing the pattern of the individual's life as *the realization of shared human possibilities.*

(italics added, p. 7)

I am trying to use the same principle in the intersubjective field between myself and the reader.

Fairly late in life I have come to realize just how tortured most of my existence has felt. That is hard to accept because outwardly I grew up in a family with all the trappings of middle-class success. Both grandfather and father served as ambassadors to their country. The emblematic eagle was a standard on the car and on the shield next to the entrance of the residence. Children of diplomats, like myself, are often not firmly rooted but always under pressure to uphold the code of the Corps: the eagle-hooded eye in my dream. So I feel shy when claiming my pain. It seems braggart, without justification. But when I listen to the endless stream of profound self-distaste and hatred of many of my patients and the way they are so closely interwoven with the fabric of their being that it is almost invisible to themselves, so normal it could nearly be over-heard, it doesn't seem so strange. These patients who are, like myself, still vibrating from the upheaval of their original catastrophes, quietly humming the tune of disaster. In presenting self-psychology theory I have repeatedly been confronted with such statements as: "So you believe in the good of mankind?" "Aren't you coddling your patients?" "What about the 87 wars happening right now in the world?" I felt embarrassed, somehow caught out. But, perhaps these critics are motivated by the need to snap the tension inherent between suffering and survival, between a life that is crowned by death? I circle back to the question of cure.

If I want to write about cure, I have to write about illness. If I want to define therapeutic success, I have to look at therapeutic failure. If I don't believe therapy is something that I *do* to you, but rather that we change and become who we are through one another, then who we aren't and can't be is as important as who we are and try to become.

Therefore trying to understand what we are able to achieve with patients means looking equally how we fail with them. When I and Ron Bodansky tried – unsuccessfully – to put together a journal on failures in psychotherapy, with the exception of two colleagues, all answered – if jokingly – that they had no failures in their practices. Since then, Goldberg (2012) has published a book, *The Analysis of Failure,* in which he describes how colleagues literally fled from him when he asked them to take part in a seminar on failure. Goldberg described his book as a failure because it did not clearly define failure (e.g., p. 215). But, I do not agree. In his "final thoughts" in the book, Goldberg writes:

> One salient feature of the study of that situation (failure) is the resistance to its investigation. Failure is such a dreaded experience that it is regularly ignored, denied, displaced elsewhere. At the very least, this book may succeed in letting failure come out of the darkness and allowing its presence to be acknowledged. One must live failure long enough to allow a personal struggle that in turn may open a proper objective scrutiny. Feeling a failure should not merely be an impetus to be rid of it, to learn how to avoid it in the future, or get over it, all perfectly reasonable and worthwhile goals. At long last, it should be an opportunity. The success of the book rests on its embrace of failure.
>
> (p. 217)

I admire Goldberg's (2012) courageous decision to write about failure and acknowledge with respect that he was the first analyst to do so in the form of an entire book on the subject. While I think that with "living it long enough to allow a personal struggle" to develop, he means the ability to finally face failure in oneself, I doubt that an "objective scrutiny" is possible without embracing the idea that failure is woven into the very fabric of our being. In my view, failure is synonymous with subjectivity, in the sense that it circumscribes our limitations and ultimately our finitude. Kohut's term for this was "Tragic Man". The possibility of living forever would face us with a different quandary; but, as Atwood (2012) writes,

> Who said a person should smile more and cry less? Who determined that less suffering is to be recommended over more suffering? I do not believe that God informed us of that principle of life. What if there is a good reason for suffering?
>
> (p. 162)

Nonetheless limitations, failure and finitude and living itself undoubtedly remain a hard road to go. The difference between my view and Goldberg's may seem like a nuance, but in essence it reflects the difference between a natural and a human science perspective. To "clearly define" and "objectively scrutinize" failure didn't succeed because it still entailed an understandable, but doomed attempt to place it outside of oneself. One cannot objectively define failure because failure is a subjective phenomenon, dependent on the idiosyncrasies of the unique, individual therapist in conjunction with the unique interplay of the specific dyad.

To illustrate the difference in perspective let me shed some more light on my dream. Perhaps the daunting figure was not primarily my own unforgiving demand on myself to cure my patients, but rather an expression of mute rage and helplessness in the face of unresponsiveness and judgment.The fears that I have felt in connection with my emphasis on the bi-directional aspect of psychoanalysis and the risks of relatedness which I have described as essential to the process of understanding and thus to therapy itself, have left me with an un-settling feeling. A deep unease of being culpable of "an allegedly neurotic *furor sanandi*" (Orange, 2011, p. 101), an accusation that was raised first against Firenczi as it was seen as "a massive challenge to the authoritarian orthodoxies in psychoanalysis and other forms of psychotherapy" (Orange, 2011, p. 101). My plea is that it is not per-fection that I seek but a wish for an understanding that I am as defined by my neediness, inadequacy, doubt, and confusion as are my patients, that I, too, am weak to the core. Or, more precisely, is an attempt at one and the same time to describe and seek relief from an understand-ing of a suffering-free professional who is able to unilaterally bestow health on the patient. One of the reasons I am so insistent on placing such an emphasis on my limitations is that I hope to lay the ground-work for the basic idea that on a systems level of discourse, it is the system that is or isn't healed, rather than what one monadic expert does or cannot do for a monadic patient. The idea that the clinician unilaterally, uni-directionally heals the patient is medical model think-ing, a natural science outlook that doesn't apply to psychoanalysis. This is what Daniel Stern (2012) referred to as "an internist's view". Maybe now we can get a first inkling of how to view cure. It is not a digital, either–or state, all or nothing, ill or healthy. It is in some sense a mess, but a mess from which we can extract meaning and a measure of human dignity, as we create a space in which the truth about someone's life can find a home (Atwood, 2012).

In my view it is a joint enterprise – a process that we must allow to unfold over time. Rather than it just being the patient's transference that develops, it is a system, comprised of the two transferences, as well as the level of implicit relational knowledge (Boston Change Process Study Group, 2010) that has to establish itself. It is not something that I possess or that is yours to give. It is survival in the face of suffering, a belief in one's existence in face of finitude, an acceptance of one's strength in spite of our frailty. It is something that must be found and accomplished together. An acceptance of suffering may have a positive side: an increase in humility. I do not believe that the dungeons of our childhood ever totally disappear, nor that the ghosts that inhabit them ever completely fade. For that there are too many states that seem like moving, but that are standing still. Trying to escape the past is like running in quicksand, the faster you run, the quicker it pulls you down. "If you think you are standing, watch out that you don't fall" (I Corinthians 10, 12).

Cure, I suspect, has to do with how we resolve the way the analyst's idiosyncratic suffering intersects, becomes entangled and embroiled with the suffering of the patient. On the level of the bi-directional encounter the analyst–patient system must be allowed, over time, to become "sick", in order that a cure may be pursued. On the asymmetric level of the purpose of psychotherapy – to help the patient – the cure that is sought is that of the patient. However, the understanding of the patterning and meaning of an individual's life cannot be found outside of a joint realization of shared human possibilities, which include the painful as much as the joyful aspects of human existence. If pathology arises in an intersubjective field – developmentally and in treatment – so does its cure. While the emphasis on suffering is a result of why someone seeks therapy, this does not mean that joyful states and feelings are to be viewed as less important in seeking cure. Joy in psychoanalysis is often, paradoxically, looked upon despairingly (Heisterkamp, 2001), or at least suspiciously, while suffering is buried in a thicket of diagnostic categories. But, just as much as we can't ultimately disentangle sickness from health, suffering from joy, can we pretend that we have the power to bestow cure, without becoming enmeshed in the basic suffering of human existence, without being exposed to our own pain, the knots, irregularities and holes in the fabric of our own subjectivity? Neither our professional expertise, our willingness to love our patients, nor even the necessity of maintaining our second row seats in the asymmetry of the therapist–patient setting (Orange, 2012) will exempt us from taking the journey through our joint limitations.

This does not mean that much of our therapeutic task is not taken up by the asymmetric involvement with patients in the form of empathically accompanying, articulating, reflecting their on-going feeling states and unconscious organizing principles. Nor am I saying we don't help our patients. We do. But only when we accept human experience, our own and that of others, even in its most repellent forms, can we return to humanity.

Generally speaking, we keep our counsel about our own suffering for good reason, as this could subvert our purpose to help. Nonetheless this does not exempt us from *silently* having to work very hard at understanding how and why we respond the way we do. We have to be careful not to confuse the legitimate responsibility towards our patients with an implicit demand to actually *be* infallible. Furthermore, in our work with patients, I wonder whether moments of cure don't also result in those deeply felt and articulated experiences of our joint limitations and failures. This by no means automatically necessitates the self-disclosure, although it can, of the analyst. Rather it involves the mostly silent awareness of his or her role in the intricate back and forth of the therapeutic exchange. Limitations in this context refer to how our experiential worlds limit our ability to understand one another, either because the need to maintain our views feels existential, or, simply because our subjectivity itself circumscribes how much we can understand and allow ourselves to feel, or, because what we feel is unconscious. If we are able to work through them, would they not also result in a triumph of shared human possibilities and the bond, thus forged through contact where it hurts, allows both participants to be carried by the experience that suffering has meaning and that pain is not eradicated but relieved by the sharing of our basic humanity? Failure is the one pole of human existence, which, if we weren't so afraid of it, if shared, could be a release from pain. Our task then is not to seek cure as a way out of our frailty, finiteness and fear of death, but rather, in facing it together, find the strength, fallen and failed, to get up again and move on.

In Orange's words: "There is no way to fix the situation or to 'cure'" the patient, so I must accept my own powerlessness to help. I must simply stay close to their experience, sorrowing and grieving and raging with my patients, even if this means that my practice feels very heavy to me. Even when – and it always is – the story is very complex, a willingness to walk together into the deepest circles of the patient's experiential hell characterizes the *attitude* of compassion or emotional availability (Orange, 1995) that the process of psychoanalytic understanding requires. This psychoanalytic compassion, I repeat for emphasis, is not reducible to moral masochism on the part of the analyst, nor is it to be contrasted with properly psychoanalytic work, usually seen as explicitly interpretive. It is, instead, an implicitly interpretive process of giving lived meaning and dignity to a shattered person's life by enabling integration of the pain as opposed to dissociation or fragmentation. A compassionate attitude says to every patient: "your suffering is human suffering, and when the bell tolls for you, it also tolls for me" (Orange, 2009, pp. 135–6). Listening attentively is itself a form of interpretation in that, "it says to the other: 'you are worth hearing and understanding'" (p. 135).

My feeling is that we may have drawn the circumference of cure and what it comprises too tightly around thoughts of achievements, goals set and met, object-constancy, self-expression, self-fulfillment, a sort of terror of health-shoulds: feeling good, being happy, fulfilled, authentic, guilt- and shame-free, healthy. What if none of this really mattered? What if what matters is that all of us are, in some inexplicable way, perfect just the way we are? Through which eyes do we see cure then? And, what about suffering? I would like to drop the pretense of getting somewhere and disregard the undergrowth of judgments that this perspective of immaculate being feeds on, thus enabling us to redefine our notions of cure. I am proposing a notion of cure that entails a different attitude towards our insufficiencies, and a non-digital relationship between happiness and suffering. For me the idea of being "perfect" means that everything we are makes some kind of complete sense, and has meaning.

It is not my intention to flat-line the difference between a human who feels more or less content and one who is suffering. It is a matter of how I see another person, that there is an inner consistency, a beauty in each human being, in which no part can be extracted or redesigned to fit our picture of them. Seen through the eyes of compassion *our* view of another human being ricochets back on us, strips our eyes to see and leaves us briefly in a timeless moment of wonder. To say we are "perfect" is another way of saying we are perfectly deserving of empathy. This is, of course, if we are honest, in contrast to how we frequently view others, in which we tally every deviation from how we would like them to be in minute judgments of failure. Bernhard Branchaft (personal communication, 12 February 2012) had this to say: "The area to which you call attention is that which constitutes the scene of intimate and reciprocal affectivity. It is the setting in which what is most essentially human finds a home and is held or dies a-borning." Our perfect imperfection being held, finds a home.

I often find myself reminding others: "Don't forget the unconscious" like some kind of Freudian cuckoo clock, not so much to demarcate a level of discourse, but mostly as an explanation to myself why I still understand so little about who I am. From time to time I get a vertiginous inkling of the limitlessness of inner meanings, radiating inward in ever-widening circles of comprehension. Sometimes I catch a quick glimpse of the fathomlessness of understanding. I dreamed of a swarthy, fat, unshaven man with a thick neck, dressed in white, a tyrant whose disapproval could cost me my life. He was sitting on a chair, playing with the latest electronic gadgets, all of which were also white. He growled at me: "Don't forget that list, especially the third part, where you have to tell me when you need to say 'No' to me!" I had finished the first two parts of the list: things I approved of in him and things I recommended as possible improvements. I was afraid to fill out the third part, and afraid not to.

This tyrant is probably an aged version of an inner self-state that crystallized at the age of 19, and that I later caustically named "Bruno". Bruno represents an inner state of cynically having given up, who has finally collapsed in the face of too much inexplicable inconsistency, bland indifference and random psychological violence. As a way of coping with defeat he developed a cynical outlook on life, tyranically insisting on a minimum of concretistic, basically physical, pleasures that limited him to a restricted level of enjoyment of life, but if taken away from him – like the electronic toys – would throw him into a murderous rage.

This emotional organizing principle, arrived at at the tender age of 19, constituting a defensive answer to a derailment in my development remains nonetheless firmly in control of some subterranean pocket of power, still exerting its influence after 46 years. Now Bruno is approaching old age, so he has changed, but is he cured? He seems to have regressed in psychological sophistication as he has progressed in age. Perhaps a better explanation would be that his capsule of power is now contextualized in a different place of my inner psychological makeup. Other centers of power have been added, other organizing principles have penetrated his pod, his demand of subservience compromised. Nonetheless "he" remains, he co-exists, reluctant to relinquish his throne. I am not speaking of multiple selves, as some relationists do. I do not mean different, discrete entities. However, unconscious decisions about how we see ourselves are made and set up as defensive ramparts against the onslaught of the complex fluidity of painful experience.

Coburn (2007) speaks about how our experiences profligate outwards and flow into and settle in some form in all our systems of relatedness. This reverses the traditional understanding of outside influences compounding into a static self-experience which then dictates behavior in the predictable manner of the repetition compulsion. Instead, it brings us back to the Gestalt principle that the parts can only be understood in view of the whole and vice versa. In other words, while Bruno is still around, he's not the same guy he was long ago. So how to cure Bruno? He doesn't seem to have been very impressed by the many attempts to treat him. Has he gotten better, or is he worse? Let me repeat, Bruno is a metaphor, not a discrete immutable self-state. He is a metaphor for a system of self- and interactive relatedness. If nothing else, he is proof that regression can't be explained by a time axis moving backwards. Rather, he has aged, he's fat now, his toys are contemporary. In psychoanalytic complexity theory (Coburn, 2009) you cannot pinpoint an experience as existing exclusively in the past, the present or the imagined future. It is more like our experiences radiate backwards and forwards as they pass through our presence. Likewise, cure does not move from point A to point B. I've been in and out of happiness plenty of times.

So, Bruno, in his glorified James Dean picture of himself, helped a shy, progressively unhappy 19-year-old get a grip on a life that was spinning out of control. Call him defensive, call him compensatory, he saved my bacon at the time. Perhaps he was a ghost that came to fight off another ghost (Atwood, 2012). Meanwhile, he has mutated into a sullen dictator, who nonetheless has asked me for help in my dream – for saying "no" to him, for structure, for guidance, for recognition. I have a soft spot for him, even if he is a bit of a bully. One more comment on Bruno: sometimes even today he is very helpful in shoring up porous boundaries, in giving me the needed edge to cut through life's petty roughness. He – like our patients – wants to have his cake and eat it, too. We desire change, but fear losing ourselves. Bruno, in fact, is a good example of how our definitions of success and failure are constantly subjected to revisions, depending on the way we feel that we live.

Some years ago, Marlon Brando was reported as having said: "You can't possibly believe you're in control, do you?" Much younger then, before life's knife had done its whittling away on me, I'd thought: "What rubbish!" Now, when dark moods can swoop over me with the unexpected fury of monsoon rains, take me from shore and toss me onto a bleak and hostile sea, leaving me with no sense of place or time, Brando's words are a comfort. As comforting as Coburn's (2009) view that – on an explanatory level – we can't be held responsible for the why and wherefore of the specific lives we were thrown into, the task that remains is to reflect on, and in that sense to take responsibility for the emotional response – on a phenomenological level – we develop towards our fate. Our past, our parents, the culture and the time we were born into – our situatedness – are not our invention. The lack of control, the sense of disorientation and lostness may then push us into feelings of guilt about our short-comings, as a means to regain control over that aspect of fated life over which we have no power. Guilt then becomes the medium which conflates and confuses fate with what we have made of it. Guilt, in this context, serves as a screen to ward off more devastating feelings. It's a difficult distinction to uphold, a fine line to walk, from which we may – like a drunk person – veer off in either one direction: "it's all my fault"; or into the other direction: "it's all their fault". Stolorow (2011) differentiates between moral and existential guilt which may become confused in a similar way. Moral guilt would then be understood as covering over existential guilt. The distinction is helpful because it delineates the circumference of our responsibility. We did not, after all, invent the whole road-show. While the burden is not, therefore, lightened, it does point us to the particular acre that we can cultivate and work on. The other area, which pertains to that which we have no control over – namely, our finitude and the fact that love and loss are inextricably woven together, also must be integrated, as Stolorow (2011) describes so succinctly and poignantly in his book *World, Affectivity, Trauma: Heidegger and Post-Cartesian Psychoanalysis*.

The phrase from the Lord's Prayer "Thy Will Be Done", could prove a better antidote than guilt in order to deal with the paradox of living. Perhaps one can look at that phrase from a psychological point of view? In the face of the mystery of life and death, and that the amount of what we know is in reverse proportion to what we do not know, the thought to let "Thy Will Be Done" often feels like Winnicott's "falling for ever" (1965, p. 58). The opposite of falling is a belief – psychologically the experience and therefore the trust – of being endlessly held. But, in the end, we are all forced to let go.

Patients echo this thought sometimes when they divulge – at some point in their therapy – that they are afraid to trust a process that ends, and us, who will inevitably leave them, like life, that leaves us all. The point I wish to make is that in face of how tenuous life is, not only in the mystery of its experience, in its brief duration and in its end, how are we to conceptualize cure? Cure from what, cure for what and cure for whom? I return to our original purpose: to alleviate suffering, we who suffer ourselves. If one paradox of life is to take emotional responsibility for a fate we didn't instigate, another paradox to resolve is that the healer is not healed. Life is not healed, it is grotesquely beautiful and terrible at one and the same time. "[H]uman finitude with its traumatizing impact is not an illness from which we can recover" (Stolorow, 2011, p. 61).

Of course, one needn't be healed in order to heal. Therapists did not invent suffering and we do not cure it. We alleviate it, no more, no less. From an experiential perspective, therapy is still the blind leading the blind. My question remains: how do we make use of this knowledge in order to help others? Because it is suffering that binds us to, or at least reminds us of, our common humanity; and it is the interaction of suffering – on the bi-directional, as opposed to the asymmetric level of interaction – that opens one path to cure. This emphasis on the painful pole of existence and the role it has in therapy is not to be understood as excluding the joyful healing aspect of our work. It is, however, the point of entry that I wish to use in pursuing the question of the possibility of cure. Suffering then becomes a bridge, it teaches our eyes to see that which we have in common. Our insufficiency, our core weakness, our powerlessness, our death and our courage to exist in the face of all of this is what I call perfection in that we are all perfectly deserving of being seen and welcomed as we are. The blind leading the blind refers to the communality of our fate and the profoundly interdependent nature and value of being seen and understood. We are all flying by sight. Cure is highly contextual, a face recognized in the flickering light of a candle. If we reverse the initial perspective of cure to failure

> a new form of individual identity would become possible, based on owning rather than covering up our existential vulnerability. If we can help one another bear the darkness rather than evade it, perhaps one day we will be able to see the light – as individualized, finite human beings, finitely bonded to one another.
>
> (Stolorow, 2011, p. 78)

George Atwood (2012) has this to say about the idea of recovering from trauma. For me, his words also ring true to a certain extent about cure, in general:

> The idea of recovery is about getting over something. I think there is no getting over real trauma. This sounds like a message of hopelessness, but it is not. Belief in the possibility of "recovery" from trauma, understood as the nullifying of devastation, is a form of denial. Many analysts, and especially those that are animated by an unconscious goal of nurturing and healing a wounded parent, cannot understand this. Their commitment is to radical healing, a transformation that undoes the traumatic wound once and for all. Such clinicians encourage the patient's dreams that their terrible life histories can be transformed and purified, that the pain can be permanently removed and supplanted by a healing experience of joy and love. Such expectations are invariably dashed, as the enduring reality of the traumatic injury continues to haunt the person's existence. There is no pot of gold at the end of the road of the psychotherapy of trauma. Under the best of conditions, a release from captivity, an increased wholeness, and also an abiding sadness.
>
> (pp. 117–118)

My dream is a an attempt to be released from the *furor sanandi*, to be freed of the golden nail in my ear, from the grip of pathological accommodation and all of my writing has dealt with my struggles to break through the myriad forms of the *cordon sanitaire*.

Basic premises: concluding remarks

The other day I said to a supervisee about our work with patients: "Look, we're going to mess it up anyway, so just relax." Why did I say this?: it's not for a lack of passion for our profession, nor am I by nature a pessimist. In part it was an attempt to lessen his nervousness concerning his first analytic treatment case. The only caveat I can add is that I've turned the corner of 65 and am thus hovering somewhere between the Fall and Winter of my life, Act V in Shakespearean terms, and that realization is accompanied by a sweet melancholia. But I would like to try to get some kind of order into the previous pages and describe the basic premises about how I see the process of psychotherapy and the mysteries of cure.

As psychotherapists we are part of a system and a process, which means that we only begin to understand what is happening as it becomes revealed to us over time. What we understand is limited by our subjectivities and the idiosyncratic emergent characteristics of our encounter with a patient. Prognoses, diagnoses, indications are relativized by the fact that we have to add three words: "with me" and "now". What we can say is that we intend to provide the conditions for the process to be allowed to unfold. We do not determine the process, the process leads us. Nor do we cure our patients, the cure finds us. Failure in psychotherapy is in one sense synonymous with subjectivity in that the topics we choose to emphasize or leave out delimit the course of a therapeutic process. Nor are we able to predict an outcome, because we do not have a clue as to how we will ultimately interact with another person.

It is very hard to think and work intersubjectively. One reason I know this so well is that I've followed closely my own resistance to the very theory that I have proclaimed as my basic stance and worked with over 30 years. I cringe from the thought that I am implicated in everything my patient does and that this has far-reaching consequences for the therapeutic process. The realization that I react to everything a patient does has dawned on me like a sunrise that has taken three decades to rise. Whether I like it or not, I react. Whether I like the patient or not, whether I find him or her uninteresting or too interesting, whether I feel bored or vitalized, excited or drained, or nothing at all, it's of no consequence, because I'm in the thick of it.

It's always been difficult for us to define cure: perhaps the concepts of pathological accommodation and the concommitent concept of the defensive self-ideal will help us find another approach. As mentioned earlier, many analysts suffer from the question whether or not they are acting psychoanalytically. Likewise, therapists of other persuasions will also question the appropriateness of their clinical actions. Candidates and experienced clinicians alike will at one time or another ask themselves whether they have strayed from the path, either because of upsetting feelings or due to the insecurities inherent in being in training, or to the work itself, no matter how long we've been in practice. The psychotherapeutic ideal seems to then dove-tail with the idea of a defensive self-ideal, cleansed of mainly painful feelings of some form of unworthiness. Therefore the first variation of pathological accommodation is to an imagined *psychoanalytic or psychotherapeutic ideal* passed down over 100 years of traditionalism: we must know, we must predict, we must cure.

The second form of pathological accommodation is to the isolated mind. The isolated mind lives in terror of failure. In our western industrialized culture the ideology that is transmitted is that every human is the master of his fate, if he or she only tries hard enough. If you're fat, smoke, aren't the early bird catching the worm, cry, feel crazy, feel depressed, forget your To-Do list, don't answer emails, don't know your present bank account status, are sick, don't ride a bike, or eat burned meat: you're fired! Weakness and suffering in any form are frowned upon and vaguely disgusting. When cure becomes implicitly linked to the "master-of-the-universe" image of the isolated mind, failure is not far behind. But as George Atwood (2012) says: people are depressed because depressing things happen to them.

The third form of pathological accommodation is in regard to our rejection of ourselves. Here we are perhaps our own most strict judges. No one is as severe towards themselves as we are, unless we are externalizing such feelings. The admission of failure is indeed painful and a constant reinforcement of isolated mind thinking. The last words before going over the cliff are certainly: "This isn't happening to me", a perfect description of dissociation. Of course the threat of self-dissolution is just a step above the thought of dying. It lurks at the bottom of the abyss. No matter how firmly one sits in the saddle, or feels on top of the world, one sigh from the beast of finitude and you're gone. So yes, we need our defenses and absolutisms. No one goes through life unscathed. The question is, how do we deal with failure, pain, loss, death? For those who have been too severely traumatized, the fabric ripped too deeply, the pain remains, or, the abyss opens into madness (Atwood, 2012). But the degree to which we deny our weaknesses must correlate with a very real felt danger, experienced or imagined, it's out there and it's in here. Nonetheless, herein lies the source of our willingness to sacrifice our inner experiences, to uphold the *cordon sanitaire,* especially in regard to our deficiencies and vulnerabilities to the false god of mastery, to the illusion of control through the isolated mind. Here cure may come masked as a felt demand to live life without regrets, another doomed attempt to exclude failure as a part of existence.

The fourth form of pathological accommodation is to our patients. Here the conflation mentioned earlier takes place. The understandable and necessary need our patients have to idealize us, to see us as strong, to trust in our guidance, our capacity to hold the lantern high when it gets too dark to see, all of this gets confused with a felt necessity of therapists to actually *be* all those things. No wonder we burn out, being in the profession of pain, the onslaught is tremendous and we may be tempted into a false sense of immaculate rectitude, believing in the myth of the healthy healer.

The fifth form of pathological accommodation, perhaps the *Urform,* is towards our parents. We need to see our parents as healthy, and by extension, ourselves. We do this in order to avoid seeing that we, as a result of upholding this fiction, have not escaped the consequences of their short-comings. Their health and ours then become linked to an idea of being cured: the relativity of parental love, for some, the absence of parental love, remain, however, impossibly difficult to understand. Necessitated by the primal need to be loved, we wrap a *cordon sanitaire* around these profoundly important humans in our lives. The imperative to cure becomes the antidote to feeling unloved. Our defensive grandiosity becomes conflated with a felt demand to cure. In my dream my scream is an escape attempt. My plea for freedom, that is for the right to be imperfect, is interpreted in a crazy-making turn-about of perspective as "fascism" by my judge. Likewise, to remove the nail from my ear is illegal.

Therapists are *Grenzgänger,* we cross borders. We go back and forth between the belief in states of wholeness and devastation. When I was in my fifth year of analytic training, completely wrapped up in the world of the inner life, it suddenly occurred to me that 99% of all mankind were not overly preoccupied, certainly not professionally, with issues that were central to the meaning of my life. This shocked me. Today I think that it's a formidable challenge to go back and forth between inner and outer worlds. The potential to get lost in either one is only surpassed by the threat of being pulverized by the tension between the two. If you ask a therapist what he did in a supermarket, he will tell you about his inner experience. If you ask anybody else, they will tell you what is in the grocery bag.

Faced with the limits of our subjectivities, the unknown of the unconscious, the inevitable clash of experiential worlds, the inability to predict the outcome of the intersection of two subjectivities, the necessity to be able to hold a developing, unpredictable and often strange process, is it any wonder that we are hard-put to define cure?

It has been one year since the first draft of this chapter more or less erupted onto the page. Since then I have been ruminating about what I feel needs to be expressed. This isn't always a very pleasant experience, as any writer will confirm. One has to maintain a position of passive attentiveness and allow thinking to evolve in its own time. I knew I wanted to write about cure. I also knew that it somehow involved the concept of failure, which I felt is related. I think the "boys in the basement", that is my unconscious, have finally let me in on the plan. I think what I need to describe is the *experience* of being a therapist, and to describe the intersubjective field from within as experience-near and exactly as I am able. It's the question of what actually happens in there that fascinates me and that I feel begs for more of an experiential answer. If it then becomes possible to draw more experience-distant conclusions, all the better. Failure interests me because I feel that there's a lot that isn't being described when we give accounts of our work. I feel itchy around too many tales *about* the therapeutic process and feel a deep necessity to keep looking from the inside out. Let's see what happens in the following chapters.

I have described my own short-comings and frailties in order to make it unmistakably clear that our own subjectivities will feed into and be a part of the intersubjective field within which we attempt to help our patients. In this sense any cure will be a systems cure. The alleviation of the patient's suffering will inevitably, if silently, involve our own suffering. This is justified because what is at stake in each therapeutic process is the search for our common humanity, as we attempt to recognize and find one another through acknowledging suffering, rather than denying it. Cure for the patient is then understood as a measure of release from captivity, an increased wholeness, a possibility of joy and some sense of sadness about the human condition. Cure is also understood as a razor's edge that cuts both ways. It shows us how intricately linked our strengths and shortcomings are, as well as what we cannot and can provide and be for one another. Inasmuch as we are able to come to terms with this, we may find ourselves released from the notion of cure, but at home and profoundly connected in our common humanity.

In George Atwood's (personal communication, 12 January 2013) words: ". . . psychoanalysis is not a task about which it can be said that it has reached success or failure, and not even an intertwining of the two, although such an image is an effort to address the ambiguity and the complexity of such things. [Its] meaning and value remain forever subject to revision."

Chapter 2

Rafaela

A case description

Most patients have agreed when I asked for permission to write about them and the therapeutic process we had undertaken. They felt that I had captured what had occurred reasonably well, and even felt strengthened by the self-object function of the written word as a witness to the meanings of their lives. In this book the first patient I asked, refused.

I have written previously that when we begin to delve into any topic in psychoanalysis, it starts to talk back to, and to do things with us that we don't expect. So this refusal was like running into a brick wall and taught me my first object lesson in tackling the topic of failure in psychoanalysis.

The therapeutic process which I will now describe – for which I have the permission to write – was not a failure. In fact, I believe we were quite successful. However, there were many times when we very nearly flew out in the curves and crashed. This is the struggle that I wish to write about, in the hope that it exemplifies my thesis of how closely interwoven success and failure are and how our limitations as therapists sometimes lead us astray, at other times, paradoxically, keep us on course. Analogously, our weaknesses are sometimes our strengths, and sometimes a disaster. Our strengths can also turn out to be a weakness in a given context. The point I wish to make is, that in our lives the fabrics of our subjective worlds are so intricately entwined, that it is not so easy to unravel what is helpful and what a hindrance, or, to define success and failure. Actually, I think that this was a therapeutic process in which my patient brought out the best in me, even if I frequently felt at my worst. Instead it was a quality of tenderness and a belief in the strength of the human spirit – in spite of my stumblings and falterings – that this patient elicited in me. I mentioned earlier that although I will highlight limitations and failures on my part, I also would like to show the deeply hopeful aspects of our profession. The best and the worst, success and failure are entwined.

Rafaela

In my waiting room sat a young man, no, a young woman, hunched forward in her chair. She turned her head towards me, like a boxer who had gone ninety-nine rounds and would go one hundred. I saw exquisite tenderness in her eyes. Sorrow lay over her like a cape, eyes under water. Then a slight bounce in her step, shoulder movements that implied a possible rapid combination of blows. I was locked in, on high alert, and dimmed myself down.

She spoke of the loss of a three-year relationship to a woman she had loved. She told me about a therapist who had just recently faded on her, when she refused to agree to a non-suicide pact. She had felt reduced by him to the theme of her "genetically determined transsexuality". That was no basis for her to work on and what did I feel about that? I thought, oh boy, she's right! I saw that she was staking out the parameters of her integrity faster than I could position myself. Freedom and authenticity based on the right to discuss annihilating herself. This was a call to arms: which side was I on? I immediately zoned out and dampened myself down. She felt her main topic was a life-long feeling of being excluded and rejected, which she had countered with flights into suicidal reveries, like others might take to drink. This astute description of the central theme of her painful past and the self-preservative function of her suicidal thoughts freed me from the shock-freeze I sometimes react with when confronted with frightening experiences. A memory comes to mind: Sitting in the back of the cab on the way to the airport in New York in order to move to Berlin, enveloped by cotton, all sounds, far away.

In hindsight, I think she was establishing her sense of agency in the face of a long history of massive rejection, and in view of the fact that she was nonetheless taking the risk of seeking help. She couldn't let herself be that vulnerable to me without an exit strategy. Understandable, when we consider that ". . . the task of coming to 'know' oneself, through experiencing being known, lies at the heart of self-organization", therefore, "exposing to another the delicate source of self-organizing initiative remains a life-or-death precipice at the heart of self-organization" (BCPSG, 2010, p. 57).

Rafaela told me her fear of rejection was so great that in situations where she felt called upon to prove herself, she felt helpless and so withdrew. Her father had said she was born dumb and would stay that way. Her mother, a failed academic, demanded intellectual brilliance and showed her disapproval with icy, silent stares. She felt caught between an inner demand for perfection, an imperative to speak only of highly relevant topics, and the fear of failure. Speaking, as it turned out, was also accompanied by a fear that I would exploit any knowledge of her. Therefore she often remained mute.

What were our sessions like? Imagine a frozen lake, so vast that the gray horizon of trees blurs with the white surface of ice. We're skating. There's no synchronicity, but our movements have a blind relatedness. We skate here, we skate there. We speak of this, we speak of that. We hear the hiss of the blades, the crack of the ice, like shots fired in the distance. Silence down below. No words to say. The fog on our breath. We sweat. She saved herself, she said during these times, by counting the patterns on my carpet. Much later Rafaela told me that she spoke of nothing but banalities for one and a half years, trust had built up, because I let her do this.

Rafaela felt that I lived in another world, in a land of hope and dreams, whereas she resided under a gray veil of despair and disappointment. She experienced my attempts to bridge the gap as mockery, as "stabs in the heart". Maybe there was a highway of gold, but there was nobody on it. She felt that I lived in an analytic cocoon. My interpretations were "soap-bubbles", "empty word-husks" whose main purpose was to make me feel good about how understanding I was. In this sense, her "banalities" *were* a perfect match to my meaningless offerings. If I spoke of a connection between us, she didn't feel it. When I didn't help her, she felt alone. If I rejoined that she had me, she said that was a lie. She was an "analyzable object", but no answers were forthcoming. "You can analyze as much as you want, but for whom are you analyzing, for the insurance company, for yourself?"

In hindsight, now, a decade and a half later, I understand why she felt that way. My interventions seem crude, carried by wishful thinking. If I was truthful, she said, I would admit that I couldn't help her. I remember the tightening of my stomach in face of stretches of silence. I recall my fear that she could make her suicidal intentions come true. I remember not knowing what to do, feeling helpless. Now I understand that, in terms of dynamic systems theory, an attractor state (Thelen and Smith, 1994; Stolorow, 1997, p. 342) had established itself, in which my analytic stance had become tightly coordinated with her worst fears and expectations. My need to help her had become locked with her fear of disappointing me and being disappointed by me. Hope was the enemy, an invitation to renewed disaster, from her point of view: damned if you don't, damned if you do. Here the two forms of pathological accommodation described in Chapter 1 become salient: the felt imperative to heal as a psycho-therapeutic ideal and the myth of the healthy healer, where the felt demand to help becomes conflated with a defensive self-ideal devoid of painful feelings and cleansed of subjective short-comings. Much later, her main fear was that the ice we were standing on *would* hold. But we are getting ahead of ourselves; allow me to contextualize what will unfold with some genetic background.

Rafaela came to analysis in her early 30s. She was born in the German Democratic Republic. Her parents worked long hours, including Saturdays, in a retail business. Her mother was an ardent believer in the socialist-communist ideal. Her parents told her that for financial reasons she had been placed in a weekly home for the first year of her life. During that period she was picked up on Saturdays and brought back Monday mornings. Human contact, she also learned later, had been three feedings and three changes of diapers a day. After that first year she lived at home, however, she was in an all-day Kindergarten until she started school because both parents had to work. Once in school, she was put into institutional care during the afternoons. Her three-year older sister was given the task of taking care of her. Her sister felt she was spoiled, was jealous of her many toys and resented having to take care of her. Her six-year older brother had also been placed in a home between the ages of 6 and 12 and had rejoined the family when Rafaela was 6. Even though she had not known him as a small child, she came to like her brother. However, he soon fled the family, as well as the country. There was a schism in the family, with father and Rafaela on one side, and her sister and her mother on the other side. Rafaela always felt loved by her father, a shy, reticent, somewhat joyless, moralistic man. She experienced her mother as an ambitious, dominant woman, given to bouts of depression. Both parents gave her the feeling that she was stupid and that no matter how much she excelled, it would never be enough. Lengthy discussions centered round what she had done wrong, never about what she had done right. At 8 years old, she began to stutter. Her mother said she talked too much. At the same time she had her first suicidal ideation and the thought entered her mind that she would rather be a boy. In school she would purposely pick fights with boys and yearned to play soccer. This led to her being excluded from both the boys' and the girls' groups. The gender issue became a running battle between mother and daughter. Her parents divorced when she was 12, later to remarry. Her mother told her, it had been her fault, mother's withering, silent stare told her that in her eyes she was finished.

With the onset of puberty, she began to withdraw. She fled into a world of adventure books and music. She hid behind androgynous clothes, suffered greatly from her menstruation. The pain was excruciating, leaving her debilitated for up to 10 days a month and further increasing her sense of profound lostness and isolation. Two events compounded her feeling of existing outside the human race, of being unworthy of love and forever damned to remain alone. When she was 17, a young man entered her apartment and under the threat of a knife, attempted to rape her. In spite of the fact that he punched her in the face and threw her against a wall, she told him she didn't care if she lived or died, rape her, he would not. He backed down, was later convicted as a serial rapist. After she had ushered him out the door, the traumatic reaction set in, she trembled and cried. Still scared to death, she eventually left the apartment and ran to a friend's house. The friend's mother alerted both parents. Father refused to come, he had to work. Mother had a meeting to attend. When her mother finally picked her up, she repeatedly asked her if what had occurred was true. On the way to the police, she walked at a distance of one meter to her daughter. For three years Rafaela said she "shut down", was afraid of all men, including, much to her shame, her father. Because of her stutter, she had already severely curbed her contact with others, but now she felt, it would be better if she wasn't alive. In her diary she repeatedly wrote "I want to die." Nonetheless Rafaela tried to break out of her isolation by joining the alternative scene, drinking beer – which she couldn't handle – and going on camping trips. Her mother said she was running with the wrong crowd. She also signed a petition, which turned out to be against official government policy. Her mother found this in her diary and informed the Ministry of State Security – the Stasi – about it. Rafaela was able to fend off any inquiries about herself or her friends in the subsequent interrogation, but she did find out what her mother – a believer in the system – had felt impelled to do. Many years later her mother admitted what she had done. But Rafaela ceased feeling anything. Alone, she trained herself to stop stuttering.

At 19 she started having panic attacks and decided it was time to seek help, first in individual and then in group therapy. During this time she made her first suicide attempt, and was saved by her father. She had felt increased pressure from her mother to identify with being a heterosexual woman, had had various affairs with men, which were mainly unhappy. She then had several longer love relationships with women. The main impediment in these relationships, even though intimacy existed, was her own feeling that she couldn't allow herself to feel happy, and would in some way ruin a good feeling, mostly by picking fights with her lovers. She noticed that she preferred an active, manly role in her sexuality and was in conflict about passively letting go.

In spite of the severe neglect and rejection she experienced while growing up, which culminated in a deep conviction that she had no right to exist, she was also a courageous fighter, a lone fighter. Thus she moves out alone, finishes high school and an academic degree without any outside help. Her sense of annihilation, however, surfaces at the end of her studies; in her panicked feeling that no one will hire her. Again, she feels she stands in front of the abyss. The break-up with her girl-friend, her unanswered questions surrounding her sexual self and the refusal of the therapist to discuss her renewed thoughts of suicide, which increasingly pull her into devastatingly painful downward spirals, impel her to seek analysis.

Now to return to the therapeutic process, in which trust and betrayal, the wish to be held without feeling suffocated, will become the central themes. The story I want to tell is how we imprint each other, leave traces that linger on in us, like tastes and smells stay in the air, the stuff of implicit relational knowing and the learning process of change that we create together. The process of therapy is the ongoing development of how to be with one another. "The emphasis that relational schools place on the therapeutic relationship fits with a large body of evidence-based empirical literature that has clearly situated the locus of therapeutic action in the relationship", and outcome studies (e.g., Safran and Proskurov, 2008) have pointed out "the centrality of the *quality* of the relationship as a whole in producing psychotherapeutic change" (BCPSG, 2010, pp. 196–7; italics added). In the Boston Change Process Study Groups' (2010) terminology, the fit that in its emergence creates a direction. The stops and starts, the stumbling along, the misunderstandings and their repair, that eventually weave us together and seek resolution in a sense of joint survival. Cure then, a razor's edge that cuts both ways in the specificity (Bacal and Carlton, 2011) required to know one another. This three-year analysis is upheld by the tension arc of the search for dignity in the face of doubt and failure for both the patient and the therapist: thin ice below and silence everywhere.

Why were we so often at a loss for words? What locked her in speechlessness? I mentioned earlier, that from a dynamic systems point of view, what seem to be predetermined structures turn out to be very stable attractor states of a living system.

> Pathology persists ... not because of fixed intrapsychic mechanisms operating within the isolated mind of the individual, but in consequence of relentlessly recurring, pathogenic patterns of early interaction – stable attractor states of the child caregiver system – whose structure is cooperatively reassembled ... in the patient-analyst system . . . thereby exposing the patient repeatedly to threats of retraumatization.
>
> (Stolorow, 1994, p. 10)

When my anxiously felt imperative to help her became coordinated with her fear of disappointing and being disappointed by me, we were locked in a rigid state and often fell silent. When Rafaela was with me she could, however, at least also challenge me to see who I was and whether I could handle the intensity of her feelings, to probe whether or not she would remain as unseen as she had been in her family. But her struggle with me was depleting and exhausting for her, so she was also often left with a sense of hopelessness.

When she was alone, this feeling of despair could converge into the spiraling-downward pull in the direction of suicide. What did that feel like for Rafaela? I imagine that it felt like being in hell, a burning sensation consisting of shame and failure: each single moment of recognition of shame triggering the next, setting off an automatic chain reaction, spiraling downward into a state of pure pain. Suicidal thoughts were a relief, a way to stop the spiral, to say "I", to say I am not helpless: every trip to a roof-top, every experience of being able to decide; an incremental gain in a sense of agency; enough, to not jump.

The most basic lesson she had learned in her life was that the safest way to exist was to be alone. To withdraw behind the walls of what she called her "castle" was to be free from degrading entanglements and of feeling unseen. Her castle, however, was also her prison. Therefore suicide would be her ultimate escape into freedom. It was a question of dignity in the face of annihilating humiliation. Much like she had said to her would-be rapist: you can kill me, but you won't rape me. Exposing "the delicate source of self-initiative" (BCPSG, 2010, p. 57), the freedom to discuss killing herself with me, remained not only "a life-or death precipice at the heart of self organization" (ibid.), but of her life itself. By coming into therapy she had expanded her inner dialogue to include me. Therefore I posed as much of a threat to her as I embodied hope. Her silences reflected that strenuous inner struggle. Counting the patterns of my carpet was a way to soothe herself.

This is, however, all hindsight. During the initial phase of her therapy, I knew none of this. On the level of implicit relational knowing (ibid.), I reacted viscerally. Something akin to anxious stomach cramps was my felt reaction to the massive battle going on within her. Had I known then what I knew later about her and about the importance of the procedural, non-verbal level of interaction in treatment, I could have approached her on this level. In Beebe and Lachmann's book *Infant Research and Adult Treatment: Co-Constructing Interactions* (2002), they describe the treatment of Karen, who in her solitary self-regulation and her withdrawal reminded me of Rafaela. Frank Lachmann movingly describes how he modulated his self-regulation, dimming down his own arousal and limiting his customary expansiveness to better match the level of arousal that was tolerable for his patient. This is reminiscent of my initial reaction to Rafaela. By modulating his voice, his tone, the rhythm of his gestures, he was able to gradually increase the affective range in their discourse and to gain a foothold of trust. He also notes that his awareness of the role that nonverbal, mutually regulated interactions and their effect on his and Karen's self-regulation only became clear to him retrospectively.

For Rafaela my symbolic interpretations and especially my transference interpretations passed right by her with a resounding but meaningless ring. Lachmann writes that "such heavy-handed transference queries never yielded much" (p. 55). Later they provoked attacks by Rafaela, as she felt I was mocking her. However, by then, in the year of our crisis, her reaction was partly due to the painful aspects of the perturbations in hitherto rigid attractor states. In other words, we were changing and that felt threatening. The realization of the "we" of the change went against her basic organizing principle of being alone.

During the first half of the therapeutic process I still often felt tongue-tied. In a variation of my nail-in-the-ear theme, I experienced her anguish as if many tiny hooks were pulling at my solar plexus. So while she felt that I let her tell me banalities, which engendered trust, I often painfully felt my inability to get into more of a flow in our mutual regulation and connectedness. Of course, I also provided space, didn't encroach on her or meddle too much when I was more reticent. It was helpful for her as it ran counter to her expectancy to be usurped. She always felt that her mother not only rejected her, but that she simultaneously "stuck like glue" to her. This example of the interaction of our differently organized subjective worlds demonstrates my thesis about how closely weakness and strength, cure and failure are entwined. What I experienced as painful inadequacy, gave her the needed room to negotiate the conflict of mistrust versus trust. She told me later that there was a rhythm to her relational moves away from and towards me: three sessions with the drawbridge up and one session with it down; two years of micro-moves towards me and one year of crisis, when our connection threatened to hold, thus placing the survival mode to stay alone at risk. In essence, she threw every bit of rejection and neglect she had experienced in life at me in the form of an understandable deep mistrust to see if I understood the extent of the depths of her despair. At the same time, each disagreement with me served the purpose of self-differentiation and helped her to define who she was. "Do you see me, and if so, will you stay?", was her question. The fighter in her wanted to see if I was worthy and this resource had served her well, even if at other times, it became a hindrance for her. In either case, it served the purpose of existential safety. The annihilated part of her wanted to see if life was worth living. At times, I was afraid we weren't going to make it, but I never gave up hope.

I would like to show how the negotiation of our limitations and failures were the very stuff of learning how to be with one another. Why do I insist on the term failure, which doesn't seem very psychoanalytic, but rather seems to have a moral connotation outside our scientific level of discourse? Two reasons: I want to describe what it *feels* like to be in treatment, either as a patient or as a therapist, and, I want to emphasize that the delimitations of the therapist's subjectivity play an important role in shaping the patient-analyst system and that this has still not received the descriptive focus that it deserves.

Many therapies fail or are terminated, not because of incorrect or unaccepted interpretations, but because of missed opportunities for a meaningful connection between two people ... and moments of authentic meeting and the failures of such meetings are often recalled with great clarity as pivotal events in the treatment.

(BCPSG, 2010, p. 3)

Both success and failure are pivotal and I hope to show how they are interrelated, both for a different understanding of ourselves and the therapeutic treatments we engage in.

At the end of the second year of treatment, our crisis began. It was preceded by a series of struggles to get a foothold into the working world. Writing CVs, trying to get work contracts, and finally finding a professor to accept her PhD thesis, while at the same time battling the unemployment agency for financial support to guarantee her financial survival, were constant replays of her early experiences of rejection and humiliation. She was overcome with feelings of worthlessness, rage. She felt hopeless and suicidal. At the same time, the very fact that she was slowly, if painstakingly starting to succeed in the world, was part of what brought on the crisis in therapy.

The other part was, of course, how she experienced our relationship. She regretted having been open towards me, it felt like being touched all over, like a rape attempt. She was angry with me for understanding her inability to talk, while she just felt empty. My focus on her made her cringe. She preferred her feelings of hatred, like towards her mother, who had only been mean to her. Her mother's message had been: leave me alone. She didn't know how to be with me, because I tolerated all her "shit" and this made her profoundly uncomfortable. It broke her well-known cycle of feeling worthless, leaving, and finding relief in feeling physical pain and suicidal escape fantasies. With me, she felt insecure, exposed and angry.

I had a first inkling of the trouble to come, when she brought me a photo of her cat, Martha, and began describing her likes and dislikes to me. She had repeatedly told me that Martha was the only reason she had not committed suicide. She had saved Martha, a stray, and had taken her in. In turn, Martha had saved her once, by jumping at her and thus keeping her awake and not letting her slide into a coma during a suicide attempt. She had also said that she had made a promise to her, she would always be there for her and that should she decide to commit suicide she wanted me to take care of her. One day thereafter there was a knock on my office door. When I opened the door, no one was there, but when I looked down, there was a cat cage. I flew down the stairs and caught Rafaela just as she was about to turn the corner. I convinced her to return to the office with me so that we could talk. We were now in very deep waters and her rage and despair were directed at me. She wanted to stop therapy.

When she left me Martha, she also left a letter in which she explained that she no longer felt able to take care of herself, but she wanted her cat to be taken care of. The detailed description of what this care should consist of was like an out-pouring of all the love she herself had missed. It ended with a plea not to abandon her in an animal shelter. However, leaving me Martha had another equally profound message. In another letter soon thereafter, she explained that no one, including herself, could help her. She no longer wanted to witness her own slow demise. She wanted to leave in dignity. She had fulfilled her obligation towards Martha. After the fall of the Wall she had felt unable to keep up with the competitiveness of Western society, had felt like a failure, and alone. I had said, she had me, but she said that was a lie. It was just my job. By leaving me Martha, she was giving me the chance to prove that "she had me".

I panicked, and in so doing fulfilled her prophecy that I would fail her. I called her and said that unless she promised me not to commit suicide I would alert the social psychiatric services to check on her. I broke the trust. Didn't I feel angry about her putting me to the test in what one may certainly experience as an aggressive act on her part? I felt shaken and scared; frightened for her, and for me. If at all, my aggression lay in the calling in of a higher authority, but it was an act born out of fear. Her leaving me Martha and my chasing after her were certainly "now moments", but of a third kind, both, each in their own way, a sign of despair. My call led to an opening of the flood-gates of rage about everything that I had done wrong. One of which was that I had not been enough of a real person for her, a visible human being, one who would also criticize her. It is true that one of the limitations that I struggle with, one of the characteristics of my subjectivity is how to express or directly deal with aggression (see Jaenicke, 2011). As we shall see, when I detail her feelings of being misunderstood and failed, I believe that her reactions were due to a more pervasive limitation to meet her authentically, or to express a wider range of my emotional reactions to her. To reiterate my premises: the subjectivity of the therapist has decisive consequences for the treatment, positively and negatively. Failures are inevitable, and can be either a hindrance, or helpful. The issue is not that I *should* have been different, or a better therapist, rather that I *wasn't*, and, what did who I *am* mean for our process together?

What we had in common was our fear, the fear of a nothingness that stays nothing, and the fear of being nowhere. The basic source of fear is dying. If we refuse to accept that we will die, we implicitly see death as defeat and ourselves as failures. We will transform the immutable fact of death into fears that we can then attempt to conquer, or, as psychotherapists, to cure. However, if we accept our transience, we may also arrive at a different view of our fear of failure, which in turn allows a more compassionate view of ourselves and what we can and cannot achieve as therapists. As frightening as the knowledge that we will die and the suffering entailed in living are, they also potentially open a path to cure. Let's see how by examining Rafaela's list of complaints which poured forth after the break of trust and which culminated in her leaving therapy.

"There were countless moments when you didn't understand me. Either you can't or you won't help me. When I said I'm at a point where I have to change something and was looking for a self-help group, you didn't think that was a good idea. You said I was putting myself down. When I said my days are filled with darkness, you ignored me, always asked the same question: what happened on that day? It's the many small misunderstandings that add up. And then when you do get emotional, you start to speak English, knowing that I don't understand a word! Why do you do that! Are you talking to yourself? Obviously! One time I said something in Japanese to you: Mattemotto, just to let you see how it feels. I think you want to keep the upper hand. It's weird how you always misunderstand or start to joke around when I want to try something new, make a move out. I think you have to feel that all good things come from you and I'm supposed to be grateful, without Mr Jaenicke, nothing is very good about my life. You always say that therapy is a mirror of what happens in life outside, but you forget, that outside no one is being paid to listen to me, and you say that the difference is that I don't have to listen to your shit. But you can't hide your antagonism. You're kidding yourself. Reality *is* different! Talking covers up the contradiction, but your actions show the truth. And you, you withhold yourself. I experienced more in two hours of group sessions than with you in two years. You may accuse me of coldness, but it's not true. I needed these two years to tell you this, but I really didn't learn anything that I didn't already know or discover myself. In truth,

I have to do it all on my own, so I don't really need therapy. If I say 'good-bye' now, then, once again, you don't react. You'll protest, say that we're 'at a significant point now' – which one? I then think – and that I 'just can't stand it, that we've become closer', but I don't feel it. But for you, I'm blocking. It's all just words with nothing behind it."

Now any therapist could have an interpretive field-day with the foregoing passage. Fifteen years later, I too, could say about my interventions, how crude, did I really say that, react that way? If we take the perspective of a one-person psychology and isolated mind thinking, we could discuss the shortcomings of technique of an inexperienced or inept therapist and the pathology of a despairing patient. However, if we take seriously that what psychoanalysis examines is the intersection of the two subjectivities involved, we will have a different approach in our attempt to understand what Rafaela said. We will then by-pass arguments about objective truth, because everything that Rafaela said is true and is a product of our relationship.

What is she telling me? She's telling me that I'm withholding, hiding myself in order to fulfill my own self-regulatory, self-esteem needs. Now we could say this is clearly her mother-transference in the repetitive dimension of the transference, not wanting to be used, to be usurped, or to experience a phony closeness which will let her down in the end. She herself will later say that her attacks served the purpose of defending her integrity, which was organized around depending on no one. But we are getting ahead of both where we were in the process and why it felt necessary for her to say and feel exactly the way she described.

What strikes me about myself is my helplessness, my fear, partly expressed in my avoidance of all issues centered around angry feelings in both of us, and in the desperate undertones of my fear to fail. The fear that I could lose her and that she could die. The question here is not did I do wrong or right, was I experienced enough or not, though these questions are certainly legitimately open for discussion on another level of discourse. The question for me is what did my therapeutic relationship with Rafaela set in motion in the deepest levels of my selfhood?; because that's where we have to look to understand my contribution into our co-created intersubjective field.

Although I have no memory of this, I was told that I lay unattended in my crib for up to six hours. I was a quiet baby. I'm walking into a hospital room. There's a fog around me that acts like a funnel, a cocoon. I don't see anything beyond a foot in each direction. I don't really know why I'm there, yes, to see my American mother, but I'm not really told what she has, it's vague, it's just one of many stays in a hospital. Reality has a spongy quality. Once, she was given a sleep cure, for two weeks she was more or less unconscious. I was told she needed rest, but not why or from what. In my early memories I see only her hands. Often, I can't find her. In grade one I beam myself out the window. Anger and conflict, as I have described elsewhere (2011) always had connotations of impending catastrophe. The din from the battleground of my parents' marriage only abated in the last year, when my mother was dying of cancer.

Let's have a look at what was happening with Rafaela and me. Let's see how my history, my limitations, shortcomings and strengths impacted on the treatment. My ability to dissociate helped me initially to regulate my rising fear in face of her suicidal fantasies and intentions. I knew she regularly went on to tall buildings to check out the possibility of jumping. In hindsight, I'm more able to be aware of the danger. At the time I fogged it out into the periphery of my concern. Otherwise I wouldn't have been able to tolerate our discussions of her suicidal thoughts.

I only gradually learned to enter into her veil of darkness, and to tolerate the depths of her pain. My silences, my joking, the woodenness of my interpretations, which Rafaela describes aptly, were all self-regulatory measures. They describe how I froze, made light and avoided my feelings. The use of my mother tongue shows the failing attempt to hold on, to connect, not to lose her, spiral down into the abyss. Now we can better understand why she felt I wasn't really there, that I was withholding. Her feeling that my appeals to our connectedness and closeness were hollow, which she ascribes to my being a professional helper, may be seen as a defense, as we so often hear from our patients. But when you look at what is behind my stilted interventions, you can clearly see the attempt to build a rickety bridge over my own abyss. Seen from this perspective, her accusation of my self-regulatory aims makes sense. Nonetheless she always saw the seriousness of my intent, and she repeatedly pointed out even during these days of rupture, that she liked me, but that it wasn't enough. She felt the cocoon I was wrapped in and she needed to break out of being enveloped by it. This is the highly progressive and creative aspect of her anger towards me and her wish to leave. She threw a bomb into our rigid system.

She told me that she had wanted to express her anger, but couldn't. She felt that that would have been a key to releasing other feelings, which, in turn, could have provided a more solid connection. My fear of anger fueled her feeling that I was in hiding. Feeling tied up, she wanted out. Here we can also see the resilient part of her isolated self-regulatory pattern. Once again, limitations and strengths, success and failure are closely entwined. We held in common the fear of being nothing and nowhere, the fog and the tied-up emotions. My strategy was to hold on, hers was to flee at all costs; both were fed by a disbelief that ties hold. Each of us felt blocked in our attempts to make contact with one another.

We now had reached what I termed the "crunch" (2011) in the therapeutic process, in our relationship. It is that point where the subjective worlds of both participants feel like an existential threat to one another. It is a point where we arrive at sooner or later in most deep therapeutic processes. It is also the juncture where a successful negotiation will allow therapy to continue and something new to be born – in both the patient and the therapist – or not.

The entire analysis had a direction and a rhythm. The direction was set into motion by Rafaela's question whether she wanted to live or die. The rhythm was punctuated by tests of trust. When she broke off treatment, we both had lost faith and crashed. After she left, she wrote me a letter describing what had happened. She had come to the conclusion that I had failed her, had "just not been enough for her", so she left. Yes, there were also positive aspects: she could call me any time, I gave her extra sessions and generally showed my commitment when she was in dire straits. She had had the wish to be hugged, but her mother had always shoved her away and her father never showed feelings and so she had learned to repress her needs. She had lost patience in the process: progress didn't count, only how she hadn't succeeded, and so she blamed herself and her exaggerated expectations. While it looked like she was sending me away, in reality it was her who left. My ultimatum that she promised not to commit suicide had driven her into a corner. She couldn't stand the pain, nor the constant lure of the suicidal spiral. She had to free herself, break the chains of unbearable feelings by leaving, by letting go. In order to protect me from any blame, she had to reject me. She couldn't bear the thought that I could witness her failure, even though she knew that I didn't see her that way. When I spoke English, she felt profoundly inadequate and attacked me in order to cover up her shame. I spoke English when I couldn't find her. Why did she want to die? Because she wasn't allowed to reach the goal of wanting to live. Her attacking me served the purpose of creating a break in our tie and to destroy faith. What else did she have to do so that I would notice that she wasn't worth it? I hadn't noticed, so she broke the bond. She couldn't stand the fear, so she left. She had also become aware in the previous weeks that she had left her castle, that she'd had the feeling she could actually make it. She had attacked me because she'd noticed that she no longer liked her old feeling of being alone.

This moving letter is testimony to how terrifying being on the cusp of change can be. Hopelessness and loneliness paradoxically seem to offer shelter. The castle of the isolated mind seems like a haven compared to the frightening vulnerability of relatedness. Rafaela had dreamed that she had walked out of a prison, the doors, to her surprise hadn't been locked, she'd come to a highway and asked a man to take her with him. He refused and she returned to her incarceration. She said that I was that man. If we follow her explanation we can easily see how she felt driven to aggressively defend and hold on to her isolated self-state, but we can also see how she was reaching out to me. Hidden beneath the trailing edge of her transference was a leading edge looking for a response. Yes, her pattern of negative expectation had led her seemingly to push me away, but she didn't do this in a vacuum: therefore it's necessary to examine my role in upholding her negative expectation. I think her anger was directed against a repetition of being enveloped by another person's system, much like her mother had done. I'm referring to what she called my cocoon, an experiential world cleansed of painful and deeply troubling emotions. On the level of implicit relational knowing I think she picked up on my fears and dissociations, therefore forcing her to further concretize her own despair. She felt that I had constructed a cocoon, which allowed me to ensconce myself in a pristine psychoanalytic tower excluding the harsh realities of life, and implicitly demanding that she subjugate herself to my world view. In reality, she said, I had nothing to do with her world, and she couldn't enter mine. Therefore nothing was happening to change her life for the better. I contributed zero. I didn't really allow closeness to my patients. I could just as well be an anonymous coach. She could read me the telephone book and I would nod approvingly. When she felt most desperate, I was silent. Therapy did nothing for her. I would always speak about our relationship, but I was bluffing, or just trying to convince myself. Or, I would ask her: "What do you want from me?" That sentence had pissed her off for two years. I was hiding behind the fact that I had no clue and maybe that was supposed to be the art of therapy, but for her, it was all just bullshit. Nothing had changed. We were stuck and she wanted out.

To reiterate: the entire analysis had a rhythm and a direction. The rhythm was set by tests of trust, and the direction culminated in a loss of trust, thus answering her original question about whether life was worth living. In her eyes, I had broken the trust, first by my phone call, threatening her with a visit by the social psychiatric service, and then by manipulating her into promising me not to kill herself. She gave the promise, but only so she could leave and to assuage me. I had told her that I had an ethical and legal responsibility to protect her and that this justified these actions. In truth, this had felt hollow to me. I knew I was upholding the letter of the law, but was missing the spirit. Actually, it felt like I was falling away from her, the more I grasped for her; an act of bad faith, understandable because of my fear. What I was now called upon to do, was to stay put, and to let her go. And so I did. That was the moment of meeting that we had been working towards from the beginning. I had to trust: no strings attached, and no net. Forcing her to promise to stay alive was in our specific context an act of concretized mistrust. Letting her go meant that I trusted her, that I stood by her; supported her sense of integrity, including the possibly disastrous consequence. From her point of view, I imagine that calling upon the state health system to check on her, may have triggered memories of her mother's betrayal, delivering her to the authorities. Extracting such a promise was too much for her. She felt that in order to stay free, she had no other choice but to leave. In the previous weeks, she had felt especially tortured by the suicidal spiral. She felt that she couldn't stand these feelings anymore, she wanted to die because she had failed herself. She couldn't continue therapy without taking the last step of saying good-bye to herself; she had to let go, free herself from the chains. She wasn't allowed to succeed, so she had to attack me. She wasn't sending me away, she was sending herself away. Recently, she had felt it was OK just to exist, that she could make it, and that terrified her. She had discovered that she didn't want to be alone anymore, so she broke the tie and lost the trust. The castle was under siege. Aggression served the purpose of self-preservation.

What I find so remarkable and moving is the differences in our experiences and perceptions and how, at the same time, this is what entailed the fit that led to the break. From a dynamic systems point of view her feeling that we were stuck was accurate. However, like most of our patients, she still interpreted this in the mode of the isolated mind and blamed herself. Let's turn now to my role in upholding the system and develop a contextual understanding of what had occurred in the intersubjective field. While she experienced me as existing in a perfect, if blind, world and blamed herself for leaving, my experience was quite different. For me, calling in the state agency was motivated by my fear of letting her go with possibly irrevocable disastrous consequences. In hindsight, I understand that I was motivated not only by my fear for Rafaela, but also by my wish to avoid an archaic fear of my own. The possible loss of Rafaela was so frightening because it confronted me with the realization that the fog that had always surrounded my mother would finally claim her. She would be gone and remain unreachable for me. Rafaela alternately defensively blamed me or herself for the loss of trust, but from a systems point of view, it was a co-construction.

So yes, on the one hand, I had failed her. On the other hand, this led to a series of relational moves, in which I was later able to engender enough trust to let her go. This, in turn, allowed her to regain a sense of agency and eventually, as we shall see, to return. The sloppiness of the process opens up the space for such moves to take place. While failure and success are a tightrope that we balance on, they are also at the heart of what happens in therapeutic processes.

If we search for that tendril of growth hidden in the thicket of Rafaela's misery, we might conceptualize her need to move on as an expression of a positive regression. Perhaps she wanted to break the chains of the past by going back to the point of death-like derailment: the loss of, the absence of mother that led to the break in her sense of self-continuity. From a Winnicottian perspective this going back to the point of disaster is an attempt at a fresh start. Of course I believed I could help her, that my job was to hold the lantern high. But what undercurrents was she picking up on in me? Why did she feel stifled and usurped by my apparently wholesome world and by my insistence on relatedness? If I go back to the moment of my phone-call I can remember that I was in a state of high anxiety, but the question poses itself: who was I so desperately trying to hold onto? The answer is, both of us. In the indissoluble unit of our mutual regulation I had reached a state where her existential question of whether she thought life worth living, herself worthy of love, had become my own. For two and a half years I had been warding off those areas in myself that didn't believe in anything. This part of me was fueled by my own attempt to run from a trauma which had occurred long ago, a mother that I never could attach to.

The fog, the thin ice, the silence, the emptiness, like a doubly exposed photograph, our two realities had slid into one. I think Rafaela fought me because she could feel the fear that I was driven by in my insistence on our connection. Having been deeply disappointed, she needed to find out if I would stand by her, no matter what. The drivenness, which I believe she subliminally picked up, must have been a give-away for her that this connection might not hold. The second issue for her was whether or not she was once again being functionalized. She needed me to decenter from myself and to stand still, to be stoically by her side. Of course she was testing me with her own conviction of disbelief and that's exactly what she needed me to disprove.

Rafaela told me that she was glad that I had refused to take her cat, had run and caught up with her, and that my telephone calls between these crisis sessions had stopped the spiral and her suicidal intent. At the same time she felt that my interventions had also bound her. She reluctantly agreed to continue, but only until her money ran out, at which point the question of suicide would again pose itself. When I pointed out that it was her fear of connectedness that triggered her suicidal feelings, she agreed. She said she was fighting tooth and nail against wanting to trust me because trusting me meant trusting herself, and she had never trusted anyone. So there we were, like two psychoanalytic Sumo wrestlers, warily circling each other, exhausted and wondering who was going to get pushed off the mat.

In the next session she told me therapy had been her last hope. I didn't want to agree with her hopelessness by accepting her decision to leave, but I also understood that she wanted to try and make it on her own. She replied: "I'll try, or not." Towards the end of the hour I asked her what she wanted to do now. She said her feeling was that she should cut the umbilical cord and end therapy, but that she might call me one day to let me know she was still here. I answered: "So trust your feeling." We shook hands and she left. A week later a friend called saying she was worried about Rafaela and that I should call her. When I called, she told me that she had understood what she had done, that this was how she always kept people away, but that it hadn't worked this time, that she had felt the connection to me. Twice she had since then aborted suicide attempts. Her letters were to absolve me from any blame. She was sad that she hadn't been able to call me herself. She had wanted to find out if the tie held and if she was allowed to stay away. These insights had come because I hadn't forced her to stay. She recalled how she had had panic attacks when leaving home because her mother had said that she was on the verge of going crazy. Our fruitless discussions of going into a clinic had reminded her of the family history of craziness. In the GDR everything was pre-programmed and not working meant winding up in the gutter.

To counteract her disbelief I had to accept her right to decide for herself. I had finally come to understand that the test of my support for her sense of agency included the choice to self-destruct. I had to believe that it was this trust that would allow her to accept our connectedness, and to survive. I had to decenter from my very real fear for her, and my own fears. All my analytic interpretations concerning the genetic precursors, the questionable premises of such a definition of agency and my legal responsibility had gone up in smoke. We had come full circle right back to our first meeting. Rafaela did come back for one more year. I will describe this ending phase of her analysis in another chapter.

In my view every treatment is an in-depth encounter of differently organized experiential worlds. The process of negotiating these differences in order to be able to be with one another is the essence of the treatment process. The fact that we do this in an asymmetric setting, with clearly demarcated roles and the goal of helping the patient, and that this setting has a definitive structure that entails the professional limits known to us all, do not change the nature of what fundamentally occurs on the bi-directional level of mutual regulation. In other words, in this sense, it is a human encounter just like any other. As such, it will always involve all the strengths and weaknesses of both participants.

From the beginning I liked Rafaela. I admired her tenderness, her vulnerability, her sensitivity towards falseness, and her ferocious battle for integrity. We were both like lone wolves, whose experience of exclusion fostered a radical sense of subjectivity. While such subjectivity provides a vital and true-to-itself source of orientation, it also has a brittle foundation and keeps one apart. The fog, the ice, the silence. How one and the same personal trait can be a source of strength and weakness and how they come to be played out in any human encounter are what I have tried to describe in the successes and failures of this treatment.

Chapter 3

Ending treatment

Rafaela redux

When we enter into psychotherapeutic processes our basic life themes will be in contact, resonate, harmonize, conflict and hopefully find a mode of co-existence with those of the patient, which ultimately enables her or him to feel better about themselves and about being alive. If we are working with someone, as I was with Rafaela, who was balancing on the high-wire of suicide, thus dealing with the possibility of annihilation, it is inevitable that such an encounter will lead into areas of myself that have experienced devastation, whether I deny them or not. Now the question arises whether I am equating the suffering of the analyst to that of the patient; am I thereby nullifying differences in biographies and the extent of experienced pain and trauma? I have emphasized the painful aspects of my personality in order to underscore my conviction that in every encounter between humans, perhaps even more so in treatment processes because there we are focusing on suffering, it is the entire fabric of our being that is involved. The confusion about the input of the therapist arises because the nature of what we do in psychotherapy is asymmetric in setting and purpose.

Case reports of patients are valid and necessary tools in attempting to grasp who we are engaging with in treatment and to open our work for discussion. But when these clinical descriptions of our patients are carried over into accounts of the process which leave out how every nuance of our subjectivities influence our patients' experience, then we have left out the profoundly co-determined nature of the intersubjective field. We have left out half the equation. I am neither proposing a symmetry of experience in patient and analyst, nor am I equating the amount of experienced suffering or trauma. It is, however, my contention that on the level of mutual influencing, the particularity of the therapist's selfhood, as well as the resultant life themes will be called forth by the patient and therefore be instrumental in shaping the therapeutic encounter. Our biographies and the specific questions that being alive confront us with will be different, but in a finite life the existentiality of the questions posed will be the same. In some relational schools the emphasis put on the subjectivity of the therapist was in part based on a criticism of Kohut's theory as a one-person psychology and a concomitant view of Kohutian empathy as a new form of neutrality, which neglected the role of the therapist.

Following this argument, it was proposed that the patient should be made more aware of – and be more responsive to – the subjectivity of the therapist. This is not my point. On the contrary, my contention is that we therapists should be more aware of the impact that our subjectivities have on the therapeutic process. This form of self-reflection occurs silently within ourselves and makes no implicit or explicit demands on the patient to recognize us, nor does it proscribe self-revelation. The asymmetry of the setting remains intact, while our role in the bi-directionality of the process is emphasized.

Ending therapy is a process. It is a milestone in a patient's development, analogous to other developmental steps such as puberty, leaving home, committing to another person, becoming a parent, finding a meaningful task in life, getting old, etc. Our task is to accompany this step. From this perspective, ending is a point on the continuum of the patient's life process. It is particle and wave at the same time, a bridge between the past and the future. The inter-subjective matrix of a specific therapeutic dyad is the bridge and will determine what is needed and what will enable us to cross it. The question whether the last session is also the last encounter, or if a patient needs to return to wander back and forth on the bridge or have some other form of further contact is also dependent on our understanding of an ending as a part of a unique process. The same principle applies to the patient's experience after therapy (see Jaenicke, 2002/2006); in the sense that we are always reevaluating our past and that this affects our present and our imagined future, the experience of a therapeutic process doesn't end. "The patient doesn't need the analyst four times a week anymore, but he needs him in his memory as someone, that he once needed" (p. 92).

For Kohut, the task was to re-open an empathic channel in the relationship between analyst and patient that was experienced as solid enough to be turned towards and include the outside world, thus enabling the patient to move on. As soon as patients have understood that their individuality, distinctiveness and otherness do not lead to a loss of connectedness, they can leave treatment on the strength of the deep conviction in their ability to be related (Jaenicke, 2002/2006).

The actual ending phase of Rafaela's treatment with regular sessions took one and a half years. If I include the post-analytic contacts, in form of emails and the two individual sessions we had in the one and half years after termination, the ending phase encompassed three years. Was this a unique ending? Yes, in that it had features that I hadn't encountered before or since in terms of the entire length of the ending phase. Yes, also in that every ending is unique, as individual as every dyad and every treatment process.

The themes that we dealt with were no different than before. The changes were incremental, if profound. In what follows I will try to describe the nodal points. While I will describe the traditional, asymmetric level of what I believe occurred in our interactions and in the inner world of the patient, I will also attempt to describe the level of mutual influencing as it was co-determined by both of us. It is my contention that it is this silent, bi-directional level of relatedness that fuels the overt, asymmetric level of the process and therefore fundamentally determines the outcome of any therapeutic process. We are neither the same as our patients, nor do we have an equal input in treatments. We are the same in that we are equally subject to mutual influencing. The difficulties that therapists have in accepting this is that this comparability may become conflated with a deep-seated fear that when we do compare ourselves to our patients – as inevitably occurs – we might come to the conclusion that we come dangerously close to being as afflicted by what we are seeking to heal as our patients are. Furthermore, if we do arrive at such a conclusion, we may fear being unable to help them. Equally corrosive for our field may be a hidden fear that only we, as opposed to our colleagues, are the damaged ones. These negative aspects of the myth of the healthy healer, a variation of isolated mind thinking, may explain why we may often be more comfortable in giving lopsidedly pristine, de-contextualized, experience-distant accounts of our work. Atwood (posted in Strange Memories, 2013) has written that he has "never known anyone with deep interests in this field who was not a survivor of significant trauma" and that we therapists better prepare ourselves "for confronting it in all its depth and complexity" (p. 2). What I am emphasizing, however, is that even if we have had less traumatic histories than our patients, this in no way will spare us the intensely personal and unique ways we will be affected by and react to our patients. No matter where we may locate ourselves on a continuum of stability we will still be responsive to our patients from that particular point and thus co-determine the therapeutic process in full measure. Health, no matter how we are inclined to define it, does not nullify being affected and having an effect. Atwood continues in the *Letter to a Young Student* responding to an inquiry about what being a therapist entails:

> The best kept secret of my field is that the healing journey of psychotherapy inevitably and always embraces both participants. If the analyst or therapist is closed off from the possibilities of personal transformation, the challenge of meeting the patient in the space wherein his or her life has foundered will awaken hatred and fear, and the so-called therapy will devolve into a process that freezes rather than liberates.
>
> (p. 2)

The reason Rafaela broke off the treatment, which was resumed after three weeks, was co-determined by my failure to hold the crisis. I didn't react with hatred. I froze in fear. The fact that Rafaela's friend called me at the end of those three weeks enabled us to resume the process. Rafaela was chagrined that she hadn't been able to call herself, although I imagine that she nonetheless played a part in reconnecting with me. I mention this because it exemplifies how deeply conflicted she was. If she had been previously balancing on a tightrope between life and death, in the sessions that followed the crisis, she teetered between hope and fear. She went back and forth between wanting to be connected and being terrified of refusal, between taking the risk of moving towards me and needing me to move towards her.

After she came back we discussed the possibility of going into a clinic. The result of a psychiatric consultation was that she felt a clinic would further stigmatize her as an outsider. Instead she made greater use of her self-help group and profited from hearing similar stories of painful existences. This decreased her sense of isolation. Nonetheless we soon arrived at a renewed standstill. In a session where I acutely felt her sense of loneliness and isolation as she sat mutely before me, I asked her if she wanted me to sit next to her. I then asked if she wanted me to hold her hand. She said no. I had felt desperately in need of breaking through her wall of isolation and had run out of words to say, nor did I have the space to stay still. In the next hour we discussed her refusal to accept my offer to hold her hand, and this time she asked me to sit next to her and I held out my hand, rather than asking her if that's what she wanted. She took it briefly and then had a fantasy of hanging herself and later hit her leg. Needing and taking something from me implied a sense of connectedness and self-worth which conflicted with her sense of isolated self-preservation and annihilated unworthiness. We have described the intersubjective field as an indissoluble unit. It is difficult to decipher the implicit communication that led to this series of relational moves. Once again she was desperately walled off and I was desperately trying to break through in a repeat of the attractor state described earlier. I felt impelled to try something new, to loosen the grip I felt I needed a paradigm shift in our mode of contact. Asking her if she wanted to hold my hand was not enough to completely overcome her conviction that I was basically disinterested in her, but it did enable her to ask me to sit next her in the following session. This, in turn, enabled me to have the courage to concretize my wish to reach her by literally offering my hand. We have replaced the traditional analytic stance of neutrality – whose fundamental purpose has always been to allow the patient the maximum amount of space to unfold – with the introspective-empathic stance of inquiry. This means that we are obliged to see how our patients organize our analytic stance. We will recall how she described me as hiding in an analytic ivory tower, as she remained exiled and captive in her castle. In such a feeling-state as in these two sessions an analytic stance in the form of symbolic interpretations would have been organized by her as lukewarm interest, or even as a form of mockery. The relational moves we negotiated were characterized by stops and starts and by highly conflictual feelings. Nonetheless they show the incremental steps we were able to make, even as they were accompanied by feelings of doubts, awkwardness and helplessness on my part and fantasies of self-destruction on Rafaela's part. One can describe what happened between us as an enactment. I prefer to describe it as "concretized empathy" (Jaenicke, 2008), arising from a matrix of relational moves.

I am emphasizing how small and interdependent the steps taken by both of us were. Even though this whole interchange was extremely awkward and bumpy, it resulted in a shift in our relationship. She consequently requested to go on to the couch and much later she told me that it was during this time that she finally began to consciously feel she could let herself into the process. Each step into relatedness was accompanied by disclaimers. For instance, when she said she felt more relaxed on the couch, under less pressure to speak and I replied that she could tell me anything that came to mind, even insignificant things, she said that she believed I didn't find anything she said was interesting. And this is how it went in the following sessions, she took two steps forward, two steps back, then one step back, and sometimes, no step back: to acknowledge the connectedness between us implied being a person who deserves being valued, which in turn meant feeling self-worth. Nonetheless, while my reply was intended to enhance her sense of secure relatedness, apparently it back-fired and made her feel more self-conscious and disconnected. Once again, one can see how no action or response, hers, or mine, is uni-directional, and how positive intentions may have negative consequences and vice versa, and how unpredictably success and failure are entwined.

In a subsequent hour, she told me she had dreamed of walking through the gates of a prison, leaning on a wall and enjoying the sun. When I commented that she'd made it outside the walls, she said she'll never get out, she would always be alone. Apparently my comment was felt as being too much of a good thing. The acknowledgment of being outside the walls implied the possibility of contact, whereas her dread was that getting out meant being in exile and in danger. Better to be safe within walls, than to be adrift in exclusion. I was moving too fast. My affirmations were then experienced as a form of usurpation. Perhaps a remark about being able to feel the warmth of the sun might have sufficed at this point.

In another session, she noticed and proudly told me when she felt that I was absent. Her ability to tell me this was surely also a result of the fact that *I* had been able to leave my analytic cocoon, and made the move towards her by offering her my hand. She went on to say that an old, close friend had visited her. I wondered whether she had been able to feel the connection to her, in spite of the absence. She said that explaining connectedness to her was like explaining colors to the blind. She felt that she had to rely on herself and that she had done it all alone in psychoanalysis, but also that she couldn't have done it without me. However, I couldn't have done it – the blind leading the blind – without her. In hindsight I can see how the source of many of my less fortuitous interventions was due to my own sense of isolation and exclusion, or due to my need to force the pace and dodge the pain. In this sense I was just another brick in the wall. It is very difficult to think dyadically, as it threatens our sense of security and distinctness. So I was clearly a part of Rafaela's steps towards and away from me. Rafaela felt she had to do it alone as she would have to leave someday and then she could perhaps no longer rely on herself. Nonetheless, as she felt it had taken her 300 hours to feel free enough to talk about her "shit" – she hadn't known she could do that because she had always just felt too weird – we agreed that it would be a good idea to go beyond the allotted 300 hours and apply for another 60 hours of insurance coverage. Now the end of the therapeutic process loomed on the horizon, and this, as we know, can lead to a resurgence of all the fears and conflicts our patients bring to us at the beginning of therapy. Her ambivalence about needing to do it alone had already fallen under the shadow of the termination phase. As we embarked on the last stretch, she wondered whether she shouldn't end therapy now, when she still had hours left. On the one hand she felt that she was a worthwhile person, but feared this good feeling could collapse without therapy. I had shown her a lot about the world outside her walls, but because she was apprehensive about involuntarily returning to her prison, she needed to stay.

As fate would have it, she now happened to see the adolescent who had tried to rape her on TV. He had been caught and was being convicted for a series of rapes. She said that it had taken her years to overcome her fear of men, but that he was also proof that she could defend herself, which she already knew then. She recalled how her mother had said she had just been lucky, but that that wasn't true. She had been able to deal with him. She remembered the song *Another Brick in the Wall* (Pink Floyd) was popular at the time, and how imprisoned, lonely and exiled by her mother she had felt, and how her sister had locked her in the basement. She had felt damned to be excluded, now, however, this onslaught of painful memories enabled her to integrate that lonely 14-year-old. Rather than feeling suicidal and going on top of a building when she felt deadened, she went on extended bike rides in order to feel herself. In her self-help group she spoke about the rape attempt for the first time. It became clear to her how she had buried her feelings for 21 years and at 17 hadn't even felt the betrayal of the Stasi incident. Working through the rape attempt and the parental rejection and denial of her reactive painful emotions had traumatically encapsulated whole regions of her affective self-experience and had led to her decision to feel neither joy nor sorrow. Her parent's disbelief and a former therapist's remark that she had "reacted coldly" to her attacker had made her feel inhuman for many years. She also remembered me saying that kids will accept a warped reality rather than jeopardize a needed tie. It was important that she allowed herself feelings of hatred.

She wrote me an email immediately after recognizing the man on TV because it felt like a stone on her chest and she hadn't wanted to wait as she had to wait for her parents, who came hours later after the rape attempt and because she expected a positive, understanding response from me. In the next session we were both very moved by her account of these events. I must have had some difficulty expressing these deep feelings because I woodenly remarked that this meant "a great gain in territory". She fell silent. She felt like she wanted to die, or hurt herself rather than feel it was "a great gain in territory". I answered that her feeling was surely a reaction to our silence, feeling insecure about feeling connected to me and then feeling that I didn't care. "Yes," she answered, "that's the way it is, it's all pointless." I said that I thought it was understandable with parents who thought their Party meeting and job were more important than her, who had just had a nearly fatal experience. Rafaela recalled how she had fled into the bathroom after initially telling me about the rape attempt because she hadn't wanted to see the ennui in my face: while I had felt close to her and very moved in this hour, I nonetheless wasn't able to share this adequately emotionally. And while my genetic interpretation was also not incorrect, one can readily see why this was a repetition for her in terms of a lack of felt emotional availability. Her terror of exclusion, on the background of the end of therapy, went hand in hand with my lack of emotional inclusion. My point is not to make judgments about analytic technique, rather it is to point out how finely attuned our co-productions were. One can see how imperfect and messy the process is. At the same time the working-through of our limitations is the very stuff that therapy is made of. Now, many years later, I can see that while I was capable of being deeply emotionally involved, the actual moments of experienced closeness were difficult for me. Much water has passed under the bridge, and I feel I am much freer in my personal life and my work with patients. Nonetheless at some archaic level an existential embarrassment can arise at moments of closeness that envelops my ability to show myself with a cloak of shyness. With Rafaela this specific combination of deep feeling and shyness led to a need to regulate myself down, which in turn, led to some manner of stiltedness. When this met head-on with her fear of exclusion, combined with her defensive autonomy, masking a deep longing for acceptance, the result was a clash of experiential worlds that either froze us in silence, or left us spinning off in opposite directions.

During this time Rafaela had fallen in love with Beth. She summed up the momentous effect of this by saying: "I don't want to die anymore." Clearly this demarcated a turning point in her life. While she was confronted with the same conflicts that being in relatedness always entailed for her – the deep longing for intimate connectedness and the terror of refusal, exclusion or engulfment – she was dealing with them differently now. If initially she still reacted with withdrawal as a safety measure when she anticipated Beth's disinterest, she soon was able face conflicts with her, such as feelings of jealousy, without running away. At the same time she was able to delineate herself, or even withdraw from Beth, without feeling she had to break off the relationship. Significantly she was also able to experience and enjoy erotic encounters without feeling the heavy weight of success or failure as her sole responsibility. This relaxed experience of embodied selfhood with another human being was a sure sign of having finally begun to arrive in herself. When we experience joy, there is no sense of having had to earn it. With achievement we may still feel fettered by questions of comparison: "was I good enough and for whom?" With joy, there are no strings attached, and we are set free. Joy is the best antidote to pathological accommodation. Her conviction that happiness was not for her was no longer a central reference point. At the same time it made her feel "naked" and vulnerable. The veil that had covered her eyes when we met had lifted, the fog dispersed.

Being aware of the enormous importance that the relationship with Beth had for her as well as sensing the reluctance that accompanied her longing to step into the light with such joyful, expansive feelings, I made another move towards her by asking her to show me a photo of Beth. In the next session she made no reference to my request. Instead she decided to wait 30 minutes to see if I would ask her again to see the photo. She wanted me to ask in order to be sure of my interest. She imagined my neutral reaction, as well as my wish for her to be the active one and that I would want to avoid giving my opinion. She wanted me to react, to draw me out of my reserve. I had failed her before, and so, as I did not raise the question again, she didn't show me the photo which she had brought. Instead, she found a creative, compromise solution to the high degree of felt risk of showing me the photo by writing me a letter. Two steps forward, one step back. In the letter she explained what was going on in her in the previous session, as described above. She added this, however: that even though I had failed her in a major way three times before, she also remembered the hundred times I had been there for her.

During our discussion of what had happened in the following session, I became confrontative. I said she had set me up for a fall and asked why she still felt it necessary after all this time to give me tests of trust. I imagine in hindsight, that her complaint that I hadn't been enough of a real person was lodged in the back of my mind. In the back of her mind were the many times I had been emotionally unavailable, veiled under the stilted mask of analytic traditionalism. It was after all true, that I had made use of the old analytic tradition of "making the patient do the work", which certainly has its place and time, but which she was precisely able to discern whenever I had used this technique to shore up the fault lines within myself. Be that as it may, the entire interaction was a co-production, heralding a shift in our transferences. What does all of this demonstrate? It shows that I had been hurt by her complaints, but also that I had registered them. The question is: why was I able to bring this forth now? When patients move into the self-delineating dimension of the self-object transference, that is, when they feel secure enough in the tie to the therapist to explore how they differ from us, such a move is based on previous countless, micro-negotiations between both participants. Thus I was no longer so fearful and cautious to disallow letting feelings of hurt and irritation flow into my contact with her, and by showing her this, to make an implicit demand to recognize me, as well as a new level of relatedness. Rafaela, in turn, after initially defensively withdrawing, took courage and wrote me the letter exposing all of her conflictual, contradictory feelings. Our move out of the safety of the symbiotic-like tie and into self-delineation was a joint enterprise. To insist on one's subjectivity would belie the fact that there are no unilateral moves. Instead we had worked our way into a form of trust that allowed conflict. It would have been unnecessary and counterproductive to introduce my subjectivity in an isolated mind manner, instead it was the result of a laborious process in which we had both "left some skin on fortune's wheel" (Scialfa, 1993).

In the next session she showed me the photo. She spoke of confronting a friend that she had felt had avoided her. She told me about how she had fought off the old feeling of being rebuffed when Beth had canceled a trip together and how she had felt ashamed to tell me this because she had previously allowed herself to show me her joy about committing to such a risky venture. Around this time she decided to end treatment after the 360 hours. She said that she "could only be on one shore at a time", that she now had Beth to talk to. She felt sadness about leaving, felt she *was* already leaving. It was hard for her to concentrate in our sessions. I felt that the pathway of empathy was solid enough between us to carry her out into the world and supported her plan, mentioning that we still had five months' time. She dreamed that she is watching TV in a neutral room. I come in from the kitchen with champagne and surrounded by friends and laughter. She feels she has over-stayed her welcome and leaves. She imagines that all contact will be over after the analysis, only post-cards will be sent. But then she adds: "The closeness to you is clear anyway. Psychoanalysis was necessary, but the parental hand is not necessary anymore." Shyly she adds: "Did you hear me when I said it's nice to hear your voice?"

One month before the end of treatment I notice how she seems to be withdrawing from me. It feels like she is literally fading before my eyes. I tell her this. She comments: "It's like watching a movie through a filter. I see the ending. I've seen people come and go and a long time ago I decided to feel neither glad nor sad." I wonder whether she isn't returning to her castle in order to feel safe and whether we couldn't find a different way of ending the treatment together. She says: "I'm sad that the three years are over." I answer: "Together with me?" She answers: "No, because the process is over. I've been on a trip around the world and now I'm entering the port. I see that my old life, family, my neighborhood are no longer enough for me. I've discovered a lot of new things in life." She's sad that this period of her life is over, and feels that she is going into nothingness. I discuss various forms of ending. I mention the possibility of writing letters, emails, or having a session at a later time of her choosing. Her fading on me like a midnight train had alarmed me, reminded me of my first impression of her as being under water, in a sense not yet born, or at least under deep cover. I recalled her basic feeling of not belonging to the human race and how we both had struggled to become real for one another. The feeling I had apropos her vanishing was analogous to someone who keeps a patient talking because he's afraid they will slip into a coma. I was afraid that I would lose her again to the wastelands of meaninglessness.

Our last session took place approximately one and a half years after the suicidal "cat crisis" and her breaking off and re-entering treatment. In this session she had an image of a fox mother biting her young out of its lair. I replied that this image may have encapsulated her fears of getting lost again without therapy, and that it might even indicate that it felt a little bit too early for her. Nonetheless, I said I felt she was ready and able to go. We also spoke about the CD she had made for me and given me in the previous session as a going away present. She felt it expressed everything that she could not say directly to me. I said that I had understood. The CD had a wide range of music on it, from classical, indie, to popular. The feelings ranged from sad, lonely, destitute, to proud, determined, playful and joyful. It began with a long piece in which one heard the timeless wash of waves on a shore and the distant cry of gulls, and ended with an up-beat, funky song called *Brother of Soul*. Just before the hour was over I requested her to stay in email contact with me as an expressed wish of mine. She said: "OK. Until the next time, some time." We shook hands and she left.

Neither before nor since have I made such an offer to a patient. I always discuss the best way of ending a treatment according to my understanding of what each particular patient requires as a result of the specific experience of the unique intersubjective field, based on what we have learned from each other, and in particular how this may be tailored to what the patient needs at this crossroad of life. The process is dialogic, the choice is the patient's. I also have had a great variety of endings: from what Fuqua (1999) has termed adolescent-endings, where it is part of the treatment that the patient leaves with a minimum of affective fanfare and there is no contact afterwards. I have had door-slamming endings, or an ending in which I felt it necessary to abruptly terminate treatment. There have been endings where both participants more or less denied that the treatment was ending, to intricately prepared endings, to endings followed by intermittent post-cards or sessions, to the many endings where there was no need of further contact. One clarifying remark: while I am open to the form that endings may take, I always make it clear that the last agreed upon hour of treatment is exactly that, namely, the last regular session. With Rafaela, however, I felt that I needed to explicitly demonstrate our connectedness, and I felt that I had to do this concretistically by making a move towards her and expressing it as my wish. At other instances I have said to patients: "you know where to find me, if need be", or, "my door is always open to you", or, I say nothing of that kind. It depends. But with Rafaela, I thought I had to give her the exact co-ordinates, the specific frequency to where and how she could contact me. This was in direct response to her statement that she felt she was going into "nothingness", that she was sad about leaving the "process". Of course I understood that the sub-text included her feelings about leaving me: a fox that gets bitten out of its lair doesn't return home. A human needs to remember that she has a home and where it is. That beach echoing with gull cries seemed nowhere.

Nine months after ending treatment she came back for one session. She gave me the scientific book she had written. She told me she couldn't find a job, and were it not for Beth, she'd felt like giving up again. She also said she was slipping back into the helper role, losing her boundaries. Traumatic memories were re-surfacing, which she tried to deal with on her own, but which she would write down and eventually give me. Nine months after that she came again, said her world was contracting, she was afraid to go out, throwing up. She feared that I wouldn't want to work with her again. We agreed to begin with a short-term therapy after her vacation and then to begin with analysis again. During all this time she wrote me many emails, which she always signed with: "don't answer this". I always answered. Instead of doing another analysis she wrote a novel, which is dedicated to me. I would not have seen her again, but in a strange, but different kind of repeat of the time she left her cat at my door, she tried to give me her novel without my noticing. As luck would have it, I did notice and we spoke briefly. Somewhat later she sent me another CD entitled "Sunday". The music was all modern, singing about success and failure, loss and love.

Chapter 4

The shadow man

A case description

Warten, warten, warten,warten,warten.
Weinen,weinen, weinen,weinen.
Wuppertaler Tanz Theater

Daniel was referred to me by a colleague whose descriptions of his clinical work I have greatly admired because of his willingness and ability to enter into and sustain prolonged periods of emotional dwelling[1] (Stolorow, 2013) in the darkest realms of his patient's inner worlds. We also share a sense of humor ever since at a conference we were caught in a downpour and got drenched to the bone. We both felt stupid and thought it was funny.

If the treatment process with Rafaela was characterized by dark tones of despair, the therapeutic work with Daniel was often set at a high pitch of hilarity. While I'm uncertain about the curative factors that were healing in our encounter, I do know that we made extensive use of humor in learning how to be with one another. In as much as 50 percent of all information given and received between humans occurs under the radar of consciousness on the level of implicit relational knowledge, not to mention the role of the unconscious, it is not so astonishing to be uncertain about what helps in psychotherapy. I can, however trace how our joint sense of humor evolved over the course of treament. One can also see how once again success and failure were intermingled in a complex manner and how humor can transport healing, or be used to mask despair and disconnectedness. I have chosen my encounter with Daniel to demonstrate that neither humor and joy, nor despair and sadness are in and of themselves a guarantee for a successful treatment process, just as neither weakness nor strength define human beings and demarcate the goal of therapy. In hindsight, our use of humor was a way of dealing with some similar life themes and the organizing priciples we developed to manage the cards that had been dealt us. We both used humor to overcome feelings of helplessness, to mask shame and to avoid conflict. Aggression was not a felt option. Sometimes the humor was a triumph over despair. Sometimes it just felt good. Ultimately it became instrumental in providing a basis for our dialogue. What I wish to describe, however, is how these life-themes immediately became enmeshed and set a joint therapeutic narrative in motion which ran its course throughout the process.

In walked a 40-year-old man of slight stature and nervous energy. He looked young and old at the same time, a strained, pinched facial expression, as if flash-bulbs were constantly been popped in front of his eyes. I felt bulky and cumbersome, by comparison. He told me he had problems with intimacy, that his fear of rejection was so great that he could imagine a five-year relationship in ten minutes and decide then and there not to bother. He felt either great or abominable. He didn't strive for higher positions because it meant he would have to be even better. His father's praise was always connected to further demands. In order to get recognition, he took on everybody else's work, felt over-burdened and angry. He often worked until midnight and on weekends. He had come into therapy because he had felt on the edge of a burn-out, and he was lonely. At the age of ten he was solely responsible for the packaging and the delivery of the products in his father's wood and metal cutting firm. If he didn't work fast enough, his father called him "wimp", or "girly". In response he threw himself at mastering every piece of heavy machinery, often sustaining injuries in the process. If held up by traffic, he got irate. He drives a motorcycle, going uphill feels safer than going downhill. When I ventured a first comment that somehow his achievements got turned into more demands, he felt caught out, shamed and reduced. He thought he should have arrived at the same conclusion by himself. At this early stage I hadn't yet understood that I was triggering his feeling like Mr It's-Never-Enough. I was surprised that what I thought of as being empathic, he experienced as being exposed and shamed. This interaction occurred again and again in subsequent sessions. I had the feeling of looming over him, like an interpretation monster, banging him on the head with heavy-handed insights. "Size matters" (Orange, 1999, 2009, 2011). Whereas he felt inadequate smallness, I felt awkward bigness. For him my empathy was a trap. He experienced my mirroring of possible ways of understanding him like a test, like an offering of a poisoned bouquet of possible answers, where he was expected to pick the objectively correct one, which, if he failed would expose his inadequacy, and which, if he succeeded, would be coupled with a further demand; a no-win situation. It also challenged a deep-seated experiential world in which he was the lonesome cowboy, never expecting or needing help and mastering every challenge on his own. He experienced empathy as a mockery of his hard-earned autonomy. "Talking to my parents", he said, "was like talking to air. When they asked me how I was doing, they would interrupt me after the third word and tell me themselves. So when you asked me, I thought that that was some kind of joke." Only much later did he feel he had a choice when I offered him my perceptions and that they might even be connected to an authentic feeling he had had about himself. On a subtle level a duel ensued in which I wanted him to understand that I understood him and he wanted me to understand that he didn't need my understanding. This is where, under the guise of humor, the mutual needling started. Daniel's self-worth was entwined with being the trouble-shooter in his job as an IT specialist. He traveled all over the country, observing and understanding the structure of apparently unsolvable computer problems, and being the expert in solving them. He was very good at it. In his initial understanding of therapy, he experienced me as competition in my role as the expert whose task was to observe and solve his difficulties; to stay in the Western movie idiom, the town wasn't big enough for two troubleshooters. Hence his repeatedly remarking that he should have known what I had said first. We both had fathers who made it clear that we were not in their league and we both had been told that we were "motherly men". With my father, I started a ten-count to see when he would interrupt me. We had learned that to engage directly in conflict led to no-win situations. Hence our survival strategy was organized around our ability to drop back, observe, offer our help through incisive recommendations, and leave. He would leave in order to escape his father's endless demands and to avoid the exhaustion he felt as a result of being impelled to fulfil them. He said that there was no nut that he couldn't crack. I said: "You mean like the squirrel in the movie *Ice Age* trying to pull out the huge acorn that's stuck in the ice and starts an avalanche?" This is the kind of humor we began to develop, in which I took on the attribution of his father, needling him with funny, but subtly derisive comments that were at his expense. I think that unconsciously he was too much of a mirror of those self-sacrificing hero visions that I did not want to see in myself and thus attacked in him.

Daniel did not expect to be understood, or even really listened to. He had a system of ordering his feelings and reactions into manifold drawers. He said he had eight topics at once in his mind that he couldn't prioritize.[2] When he talked to me, he would start in a circular fashion working his way to the center of the point he wanted to make. Sometimes I had no idea where he was headed, other times I thought I could see where he was going from a mile away. In actuality his way of talking was just a step removed from the endless internal brooding he subjected himself to. This could be conceptualized as an obsessive way of thinking and speaking. Brandchaft, however (Brandchaft *et al.*, 2012) has redefined such an internal debate as a part of a system of pathological accommodation, in which one is constantly justifying oneself towards the browbeating of originally alien voices that have become a part of oneself, voices that must be appeased at the price of self-negation. In the beginning stage of treatment I found myself listening to him up to 45 minutes without comment. I was, however, becoming unhappy with this state of affairs. I felt antsy, irritated, but remained mute.

With Daniel I initially had no idea why I felt immobilized; certainly I wasn't sitting on my chair ruminating about what I later came to recognize as my brother transference. I think what eventually spurred me into action was my feeling of being out of contact with him and lost. My ability to wait and listen to patients for long periods of time is, of course, standard fare for any therapist, as is the capacity to stay out of their way. However, going beyond the necessity and purpose of the asymmetric stance, this ability was also fueled by my transference. My virtue is my vice, and vice versa. I had been locked in a kind of clinically sanctioned stupor, whose hidden essence in this particular situation was to forfeit any input of my own in order to maintain the peace.

So there I was with Daniel, locked in the same way that I had organized my experiences with my brother; a brother transference that had apparently survived five decades and hundreds of hours of psychotherapy of diverse schools, years of clinical training and practice. What am I to make of this? The common belief that all therapists have at least one screw loose comes to mind. And certainly it is true that we have suffered the sin of believing our own malarkey when it comes to upholding the myth of the healthy healer; or, more precisely, when we have embraced clinical approaches that would mitigate or exclude the effect that our own subjectivity has on the psychotherapeutic process. In 1979, Atwood and Stolorow presented the analytic world with their book *Faces in a Cloud: Subjectivity in Personality Theory*, in which they described how the subjectivities of four prominent psychoanalysts – Freud, Jung, Reich, and Rank – were closely entwined with the subsequent theories that these gifted thinkers developed. Hence they came to the conclusion, that what psychoanalysis needed was a theory of subjectivity itself. Out of this they later developed the theory of intersubjectity.[3]

What does this mean about the efficacy of psychotherapy and any notions we may have about healing? It says this: that each new patient we encounter will trigger aspects of our subjectivities in unforeseen ways that will necessitate a renewed, silent self-reflection. Otherwise we will block our ability for emotional dwelling, our capacity to emotionally lean into, participate and understand the inner states of our patients (Stolorow, 2013). We will remain locked in our old patterns of expectation, self- and interactive regulation.

So sat the expert, the younger brother, listening mutely to Daniel. My brother is one and a half years older than I. He is one of the people that I have loved most deeply in my life. He shielded and pro-tected me from a world that I experienced as profoundly dangerous. He opened many worlds for me: art, music, literature. I was often carried by his passionate views about life. At the same time, there was a price. I was not allowed to question or challenge our roles. As boys this meant that I was not allowed to win in any competition or game we engaged in, until I was physically bigger than him at age 11. "Size matters" (Orange, 1999, 2009, 2011). If I challenged him, ret-ribution followed. My parents, however, also cruelly punished my brother, attempting to break the spirit of a vital boy. Dimly I knew this and it broke my heart. Thus I was thrust into a deep conflict of loyalty. I could not sell him out. So I held still, in order to preserve some kind of peace. This pattern of behavior was so deeply engrained that it took me well into my fifties to win guilt-free at competitions, such as a game of tennis, with good friends. Team sports allowed me to shine without the danger of stepping alone into the limelight. In grade eight, captain of my football team, I threw the game, rather than win against a team headed by my best friend.

With Daniel there were confusing role-reversals. I was physically bigger than him, which made me feel awkward and constrained, aside from the issues he himself had with size. I didn't want to repeat that advantage, such as my brother had. On the other hand, in my role as therapist, I was by definition in the back seat. By virtue of the same role, I was responsible. Therefore I had to act. Daniel expected me to act. In fact, in his view, as I later learned, I had 44 packages that I would dole out sequentially for him to therapeutically work through. I was to offer him a new, more efficient ordering system which occluded his own and all would be well. An understandable longing for the guidance of a benign father-figure, which would have remained oppressive inasmuch as it would have excluded a dialogic search for finding his own distinctness and authentic voice. The isolated mind of the expert therapist would replace the isolated mind of the patient, by-passing the need for contact and relatedness. Lash LaRue encounters the lonesome cowboy, or, as he referred to himself, the "shadow man", a stand-off. Here it becomes clear how early in the process our life-themes became entwined and were set on a mutual course, with the opportunity of a new resolution, or a repeated failure, for both participants. Two men, used to working in obscurity and alone, must find a way to step into the light. Humor helped us to resolve the stand-off. For instance, when he told me about the 44 packages, I asked him how old he was. He said: "Forty-three." I said: "So, one more to go." I think we used ridiculousness as a felt guerilla tactic to break out of hierarchically oppressive systems; in this case, a system which we had recreated ourselves. An attractor state in which I felt my analytic stance, dove-tailing with my unconscious transference, demanded that I had to endlessly listen and he felt afraid that he couldn't get through to me, therefore my silence only exacerbated his tendency to perseverate. From very early on in treatment and before we found other ways, humor served the positive purpose of disrupting a frozen analyst–patient system, giving us the space to look for new ways of organizing our experience.

How did Daniel come to be the shadow man? With a father who treated him – in Daniel's words – as an "employee" from the age of 6 and a mother who either vanished into her garden or came into his bed to shed tears over the authoritarian behavior of his father, the young Daniel took to wandering off on his own in order to escape them both. In his wanderings he would seek out risks and suffered many accidents. Most likely this was a way to feel alive and confirm his existence, as someone who didn't need what he couldn't get, and unconsciously to concretize his sense of suffering through pain. He remembers fainting from an electric shock and upon opening his eyes seeing everyone stand around him. He thought: "So this is what it's like to feel at home." There was some sense of home through the fact that it was a large family. The grandparents lived with them and provided the parental care the parents who were preoccupied by survival struggles could not. Daniel remembers fondly communal Saturday TV nights and shared meals. Although these gatherings involved contact, there was no communication about how anyone felt. He has two older sisters, one who is "a bit reactionary" and somewhat morose and who followed in their father's footsteps in the firm. Too old to allow the development of a close relationship, she nonetheless sometimes helped Daniel with his school work. The other sister, who is spunky and vivacious, was the closest and most supportive of his sibling relationships. His older brother, also a loner, was a play-mate for him. The most sensitive of the children, he later developed a dissociative disorder and still lives and works at home. Aside from the strain imprinted upon the family by the insolvency struggle, there was also the pall left by the tragedy of the death of a brother, who died at the age of 2, due to a misdiagnosed heart condition. This trauma was never discussed. While we as therapists try together with our patients to reconstruct how it specifically was for them to grow up in their families, we do well to remember that all of us just do the best we can, even as we fail. This family, like so many, was trying to stay afloat and much was neglected by this struggle. Much was sacrificed in the service of functionality and achievement. In particular it was the lack of the possibility for affective contact, the absence of a relational home for painful feelings, the lack of space for the exploration of inner experiences, which led to Daniel's basic organizing principle of feeling alone and adrift at sea.[4] This can, however, only be understood within the wider context of the ubiquity of human suffering expressed in the specific situatedness of our past.

In grade school he was bright and the class clown. Against family resistance he applied for and was accepted into the highest educational track, the Gymnasium. Coming from a background in which the entire family worked in the struggle to maintain the family business, he was unprepared for the language, the mores, and the exclusive cultural self-assurance of his upper middle-class school-mates. Futhermore the family business had faced insolvency and had poured all its energies into getting back on its feet and eradicating the shameful spectre of failure in a small town where every change in status was closely registered and judged.

Feeling abandoned by his parents, ostracized by his home town and school, his grades became erratic and he was demoted to a less socially prestigeous school system, the Realschule. There he was once again rejected as the head of that school resented being the catch-all for "Gymnasium rejects". For the Gymnasium crowd he wasn't the right class. For the Realschule, a failed snob. Thus he found himself humiliated to be in the least demanding school system, the Hauptschule. For his family, he was the black sheep, his father said he would bring them all into jail. His father hit him with a belt, chased him to the cellar stairs until he fell. In the first dream Daniel told me, Daniel was responsible for a herd of sheep. When a black sheep went astray, he was forced to choose who he would save, the herd or the stray. He chose the herd, sacrificing the black sheep. Humiliated and shamed in and outside his family, Daniel became furious and decided to become the master of his own fate. With tremendous courage and tenacity and without any outside support Daniel worked his way up the hierarchical school system until he reached the highest level, the university. As a child he had already learned to rely solely on himself. From the traumatizing school experience of rejection and exclusion, which left him feeling annihilated, the shadow man was crystallized as the lone fighter, who, by keeping a low profile and relying on no-one, would achieve his aims. He had only one goal: to get a ticket out of a past, which, in his eyes had done everything to stop him and nothing to support him. In terms of similar life themes, a drawing comes to mind that I made as a child as part of a psychological test. I am seated high on the branch of a tree, while the rest of my family picnics below. In her book about the role that sibling relationships have in pathological development, Adam-Lauterbach (2013) describes how the middle position of children can lead to a feeling of exclusion. The survival tactic that follows from this organizing principle is the necessity of getting away from the reality of never arriving.

Daniel studied with a kind of silent fury. In order to finance his studies he worked in the mornings for the ambulance service of the Red Cross. His co-workers did not like to accompany him, because he always seemed to be on call when the worst accidents happened. For Daniel, the job was an eye-opener. He said he saw the worst and the best of what can happen in life and that he had learned much about death and helplessness, but also about gratefulness. In the afternoon, he went to classes and studied. In the evenings he was engaged in student government organizations. He had good friends, but little time for social activities, or deeper relationships with women. At semester breaks he worked in his father's firm. He finished university with two diplomas. Between diplomas he worked a year in England. He entered a big firm, left because the structures were too rigidly hierarchical, then found a job in the renowned company he still works for. During this time he had several relationships that petered out with the waning of sexual attraction. For a while he lived with a couple. Both are his friends. He had the role of confidante with the wife. When they got divorced he had a brief affair with her. Later he became the godfather of their child. In these years before entering treatment he worked excessive hours, frequently felt overburdened and exhausted.

In the first year of treatment Daniel was involved with a woman, Katja, who was on the rebound from a disastrous relationship. While his relationship with her was fueled by exciting sexual encounters, emotionally their contact was circumscribed by Daniel's usual role as helper. He moved her furniture and listened for hours to endless diatribes about her disappointments in life. He became aware of and frustrated by his attempt to gain recognition and to widen their emotional contact by primarily being of service to her. When I ventured a mother transference interpretation, where he had also been the catch-all for grievances in exchange for attention, he became irate and rebellious towards me, but it also freed him to express his dislike of his girl-friend's negativity and to demand a more equal partnership.

In a further attempt to break out of our rigid attractor state, I interrupted a 45-minute monologue, saying that I felt out of contact and cut off. He initially reacted to this relational move on my part by reading one of my books to see what it was that he was doing wrong. I could see that he had reacted in his habitual way by drawing all blame upon himself and trying to correct the conflict by a solitary act of self-improvement, rather than going into a more direct contact with me. Nonetheless it was *my* book that he had read and therefore it had been an attempt to reach me. As I have pointed out, confrontation is difficult for me. The Lone Ranger acts under the cover of night. Being in the light makes me nervous. Therefore I answered by saying that I hadn't been all that happy about my intervention. But he said that it had been helpful because it had structured him. These interactions exemplify how on the bi-directional level of our contact, we were both struggling to free ourselves from transferences that locked us into solitary, isolated modes of organizing our experiences of one another and that, in our encounter, had been transformed into a stagnant patient–analyst system; I hadn't been satisfied with my intervention because it had somehow felt abrupt, heavy-handed and had had an accusatory undertone. Now, it is clear to me that, on the one hand, the spirit it was made in was not one of an inquiry as to how we had gotten ourselves into this predicament. This was my part of his feeling that he had done something wrong. On the other hand, it can also be said that rigid attractor states need perturbations in order to open them up for re-organization.

Much later, when we spoke about the beginning phase of our process, he told me that he had initially reacted to my responses as if I had been lecturing him. He dealt with it combatively as a task that he had to work through, that is, as familiar territory: another nut to crack. In Daniel's words: "I talked and talked in the hope that you would finally give me a task. I wondered, what else does he want to hear? And then after all my talking you would say *one* sentence. That was like being hit by a baseball bat. I mean, one sentence! I came here with either fearful or soothing feelings, black or white. But your precise differentiation, the constant mirroring and naming of my feelings and characteristics were helpful. And by reading your book, I understood that the purpose of all that mirroring was to bring my feelings into a context. In hindsight that was a helluva nut! The ability to connect my experiences with how I am, opened up the possibility of choice. Before, I only thought about tasks, at work and in relationships that had to be fulfilled. That you listened to me for such long stretches of time also made me aware that that's exactly what I did in my relationships. That must have been pretty gruesome for you. I noticed that it pissed you off, but I didn't have a clue what you meant when you said you felt cut off, because listening endlessly was always what I did with everyone else. But with you, it was only half an hour that you had to listen." He thought that was pretty funny, so did I.

On the asymmetric level of my participation it was, as we have always known, the listening, the understanding, the bringing into language, the empathic tracking of Daniel, the emotional dwelling in his experiential world, that was therapeutically helpful. I feel grateful and assured by the efficacy of the empathic-introspective listening stance and the asymmetric setting and I am in awe of Daniel's ability to make use of and concisely speak about his therapeutic experience. At the same time, I wish to emphasize my conviction, as I have throughout my work that all theoretical and clinical approaches pass through the filter of our idiosyncratic subjectivities, which can only be understood within the unique intersubjective field we experience with our patients. Therefore, I return now to the therapeutic process with Daniel, to continue to describe the interplay between the asymmetric and bi-directional levels of discourse.

Following the confrontational sessions which established a new level of contact between us, Daniel cried for the first time during his analysis. He said that he repeated himself because he didn't believe the other person heard him and that he was aware that he had a problem trusting relationships. He felt that he was everyone's garbage pail and that he was just happy to get a new bag-liner so that he could continue to swallow. He was afraid of his feelings, his neediness, which would either swamp the other person or dissolve him. He was distressed that for him to show need or feeling was tantamount to being weak. He remembered sitting at his beloved grandfather's bed when he was dying and being the only one in the family to notice the moment his grandfather died. "Everyone else," he said, "was talking about how to dispose of him." His shame in reaction to being understood, or receiving support in any form was connected to his feeling that showed he needed help which, in turn, proved his basic inadequacy: "As if I was a dry sponge which got one drop of water." He fell into a spiral of shame, in which he regretted not having been able to accept what people had offered him in the past. His sadness, expressed and held, however, became the medium for him to reconnect to himself and he mourned the profoundly ignored child he had been. This is a good example of how developmental trauma is not expunged, rather, through finding a relational home, it can become integrated and lead to a feeling of increased wholeness in the patient. A sense of sorrow remains. He stopped trying to save Katja, was amazed when he, without even trying very hard, was able to get an excellent rating in a training session at work. He stopped pushing people away he didn't like; nor did he idealize those that he was fond of. The idea that he might be "enough" replaced the conviction that he was "Mr-Never-Enough". In my office, he resisted opening the door for other patients.

I have described how Daniel and I had gotten ourselves into a rigid attractor state in which I felt imprisoned by my listening stance and Daniel felt locked into a hopeless attempt to make himself understood. Daniel came to sessions feeling either fearful or soothed. In general, he experienced two basic states: strenuous striving or exhausted dreaming. I commented that this seemed comparable to the digital computer world of either-or, zero or one. There was no in-between, no integration of feeling states and no hope of communication and joint exploration. It was a hermetically sealed-off system in which we faced each other in the afore-mentioned duel of monads. Fortunately, we discovered that Daniel's digital states corresponded to his experiences of his father, on the one hand, whom he referred to by his first name, Hubert, and, on the other hand, to his cherished grandfather, Albert. Daniel began to place his father on his right shoulder and his grandfather on his left shoulder, in a mock parody of devil and angel, as a way of orienting what he felt. Picking up on his humorous playfulness, I suggested a role-playing method I had learned from Gestalt therapy, and proposed that Hubert and Albert should have a talk. I placed my waste-paper basket in front of Daniel and asked him to assign the roles. Tellingly he assigned Albert to the waste-basket and he would take on the role of Hubert. Tellingly because he described Albert as being somewhat Buddha-like, at peace with himself, but also the silent tolerater of suffering, the soulful dreamer. Daniel spent happy hours in Albert's tailor workshop, quietly assisting his grandfather in a twin-ship manner, enjoying a feeling of essential, undemanding and silent likeness, whereas Hubert made impossible demands, paralyzing Daniel and spurring him into a hyper-activity in order to get free. The question became how to integrate the doer with the dreamer, the dictator with the Buddha, the functional with the felt aspects of Daniel's experience. Whenever Daniel/Albert said anything vaguely positive about what he had done or found enjoyable about his life, Daniel/Hubert would bark: "Why didn't you do that sooner?", or, "So what?" Daniel said he felt like two people. Whatever he expressed, another part of him relativized it. Whenever I mirrored a feeling of his, he thought: "What the hell does he want from me?" Daniel would literally stop breathing, hold his breath. He told me he felt paralyzed then, in shock, a gaping emptiness enfolded him. He didn't know what he felt. I said: "Breathe." The holding of his breath followed the feeling of shameful exposure mentioned earlier. The shame was the result of my having named a feeling or need. In essence, he was ashamed of even having a need. The construct he had is that everything is relative, or that whatever he said corresponded to an objective, universal truth. Often I would then offer him a humorous image. This gave him a valve for the immense inner pressure he felt. "Your humor was tremendously helpful for me because it came at a point when I was stuck, although I could imagine that some of your comments or jokes could be difficult for others. For me, they were a relief, took out the heaviness, the burden of cracking the nut." Because Daniel's world had largely been a reactive one, in which he lived in a terror of accommodating to objectively "true" criteria and "justified" demands, humor allowed us a way to joke about serious things.

Humor, like joy, became the antidote to pathological accommodation for both of us and exploded the rigid attractor state that had held us captive. Daniel said: "It helped that we have the same sense of humor." I said: "Yeah, for the sense of the absurd, especially when we feel powerless." "Yes, but an admitted powerlessness, not fatalistic, but accepting that the freakiness is also part of who we are, and, anyway, it's fun," Daniel answered. The sense of humor we shared was the result of how we had similarly organized our worlds. On one level it was a defense against a felt helplessness, a dodge around opposing forces we felt inferior to, and unable to confront. It was a denial of a defeat suffered long ago, a shrugging off of weakness in an attempt to escape pain and avoid loss. There was, however, a development over how humor was used and it paralleled the intermingled working-through process of our life themes. If at the beginning of the therapeutic process, humor masked the duel of the monads that eventuated in a locked analyst–patient system, it evolved into a mode of dialogue that allowed us to free ourselves from the similar crushing organizing principle, the fear of exclusion. If initially Daniel experienced my interventions, my naming of his feelings like hammer blows he had to ward off, and I felt like a bull in a china shop, this subterranean, aggressive confrontation developed from a needling repartee into a liberating shared sense of humor. The humorous comments allowed Daniel to see how he side-stepped his needs, without feeling shamed. They allowed me to use humor not as an avoidance of confrontation, a denial of weakness, but as a potent mode of self-expression. And it allowed us to come out of a less ghost-ridden form of contact and move into the light.[5]

Daniel initially experienced my empathy as pedagogic and reacted combatively by organizing my interventions into nuts to be cracked. My usage of humorous pictures as a way of naming and contextualizing his experience was pivotal in his feeling understood. If I had offered him sober accounts of causalities he would have shrugged his shoulders. When friends had done this, he told me, he would file it under the heading "esoteric". If, however, I responded to an expression of fear on his part by saying that the monster behind the bush is always a lot bigger than the one you can see by naming it, he felt relieved and could join me in an exploration of what he was afraid of. Or, if I referred to him as the "shadow man" in response to his way of operating as an *éminence grise*, while hiding his own agenda, he immediately understood. His feelings were like a foreign language for him, but the pictures undid a knot and allowed him to develop his own pictures. He would then imagine how the "shadow man" slowly slinks through the fog, carefully, his head ducked down. This freed him from the digital, guillotine-like mode of ordering his feelings and opened up a space within which he could explore himself. Concrete explanations were also helpful. For instance, if I explained the primacy of subjectivity in the image of "I-am-a-camera", whereby each of us "films" the world in a highly idiosyncratic manner, this broke up the deadly struggle between Daniel/Hubert and Daniel/Albert. Introducing Gadamer's idea of a dialogic truth helped Daniel to feel that one could have different perspectives and yet arrive at a common understanding. What was I doing? I had certainly left the narrow path of traditional interpretation, but I had done so on the basis of a dialogically-informed empathy. Together we had transformed his habitual use of packaging his feelings according to outside standards. The use of pictures was a form of containment, which gave him the frame in which to paint his own pictures. This mode of structuring himself opened the Gestalt and gave him the freedom to define himself, whereas before he thought he had to invent himself according to what he felt was demanded of him. The 44 packages he imagined I would thrust upon him and which he had to comply with were slightly more benign, but nonetheless a repetition of Hubert's demand for compliance. The humor and the pictures gave us a dialogic platform to explore what it meant to be Daniel. Discussing this, I ventured that he took my pictures home like nuts, opened them and then developed his own pictures. "No," he said, "I wrote stories about them." "Your own!" I said. "Yes, but if we hadn't had the humor, I would have gone into the hole of depression. One has to have a way to look up and beyond." "Otherwise, you'd have stayed buried under," I answered. "Yeah, it doesn't get any lighter down there. You would comment on something and then I would correct and correct and correct." I started to laugh because I found it humorous how I thought he was describing my bumbling attempts to understand him. But he said: "No, no, no. It was helpful when you kept asking how I felt and when you offered me bits of theory. Then I would go home, look it up and think about it. That was a nut, but it was one that I wanted." "So the pictures, the theory helped to develop your own images." "Well, at least they were like a flash-light."

Daniel began to wonder how I "can stand it with him". But he also felt connected, enjoyed our laughter and felt like he was getting something from his analysis, as opposed to his old feeling that he should be able to do it all by himself. At the same time he was sad about the 36 years that he felt it was forbidden to state his own needs. Daniel now could feel when he was hungry or tired. He used to change his clothes according to the calendar, rather than according to how he felt or what the weather was like. He began to think about his relationships with women. He separated from the woman who was abusing his accommodating side. There was another woman, Irene, with whom he has had a close and friendly relationship for many years. He asked himself why this relationship had not moved onto a more intimate level. He felt that he was in a brother role with her and that he would be a "victimizer", a dictator like his father if he wanted more from her. When he let Irene know that he would like to have children one day and also that he had missed her while he was gone over the weekend, she responded by saying that men only want children to mirror their egos and that women become nothing more than vessels. This view of men towards women actually closely resembled his father's view of women. This clarification freed Daniel, but left him stymied, exhausted and still. In the session following this disillusionment, he went into his "hand-puppet mode", speaking quickly, disregarding his feelings.

Subsequently Daniel spontaneously moved onto the couch. He felt stuck and wanted to tackle more difficult issues. It relaxed him to be in his own space. He became aware about how strenuous relating is for him and he felt bad about it. He told me about how deeply embarrassed he had been with Irene, when he hadn't known the meaning of a medical term she mentioned. His past failures and the feelings of humiliation he had undergone at school roared up from the depths of his past and washed over him. He immediately went into his "hand-puppet" mode with her, doubling his efforts to be there for her, and vanishing behind the scene. He understood how this work-mode was a way for him to structure contact and avoid the "free-falling feeling". "I *must* know, I *must* give an original answer, I am the 'response-machine'."

I allowed myself to drop into that dark space. Banks of flood-lights suddenly came on and I couldn't possibly live up to the demands of all the eyes directed at me. Anxiety made my skin crawl; ate at my stomach. A feeling of not wanting to be here, or anywhere, arose. A profound sense of weakness opened a huge gap between myself and the world, as well as an overwhelming hopelessness towards ever being able to fulfil the strain of bridging that gap: a second in the day of the life of a therapist facing the rubble of destruction in our patients and ourselves.

In terms of similar life themes, an automatism to step back into the safety of shadows remained operative in both of us. Going onto the couch, however, allowed Daniel to be alone in the presence of the other (Winnicott, 1965). It increasingly muted the "response-machine". The "hand-puppeteer" took a holiday and for a while. Daniel fell silent. Tears came and went like clouds passing by. Sorrow arose, but it covered him like a blanket. This was new for us. We had been used to riffing off each other. Now, this silence! It did not come easy. The image of the response machine fitted me like a glove, as well. I had to go through a kind of withdrawal from our humorous repartee. Scenes with my brother floated through my mind. We had to write an essay on Racine for the French Lycée we attended. We had gone into fits of laughter about Racine's rhymes, such as "gloire" and "croire"; the two of us racing down rainy, wind-swept streets of Paris on a motorbike. No helmets. These memories comforted me and I fell still.

Such is the seeming paradox of psychotherapy, that Daniel's new-found ability to allow his sadness and our joint capacity to shift down into a state of quiet communion and contact, led to Daniel being able to be more aggressively assertive and successful in his job. This of course brought Hubert onto the scene in terms of fears of dire conse-quences, but less than before. When I commented on his expansive-ness, he said: "That paralyzes me." "You can't hear it?," I asked. "No, I deny it. But I do show myself more. I notice others have similar feelings. That takes away from my specialness. Still, I'm actually interested in other people and go into contact with them. I'm just beginning to discover the human world around me. I used to judge everything cognitively; feelings were a source of error. The world was full of people who could damage me. Anything positive bounced right off me. I played possum. I had to turn my feelings off. Otherwise I would have always felt scared." His loss of "specialness" was due to the fact that his self-esteem was no longer so entwined with his self-abjuration. The integration of his painful feelings of smallness lessened the need for defensive grandiosity. The two states became less dissociated. In his words: "I used to feel like a Grand Seigneur because everyone came to me for advice, but I hadn't noticed my wishes were never of interest."

In terms of similar life themes, the conscious groundwork for my becoming a therapist was laid at the age of 20, when I found myself listening to everyone's problems at college. Curiously, I would respond more on the basis of implicit knowing, than logical reasoning. This mode of responding entails both my weakness and strength and most likely goes back to the pre-symbolic way that infants scan their mothers' faces. I was able to feel what others felt without the use of symbolization. Like Daniel, I often experienced strong feelings as subjectively dangerous and regulated high states of arousal down. Taking the back seat thus became natural for me, while opening up space for others. By virtue of the same characteristic, my wishes were secondary. Interestingly *Bruno* (see Chapter 1) made his appearance at just about the same time. *Bruno* was a defensive rampart against crushing experiences of meaninglessness, which he countered with sarcasm and by falling back on physical sensations as a way of vitalizing a threatened sense of selfhood.[6]

In a following session Daniel was proud of the fact that he hadn't immediately started the response machine with people anymore and that "the garbage pail wasn't even a quarter full". The next day Daniel said he was moved, that something had happened for him in the session the day before. He had done something well and said so to me. When I didn't give him a "don't-over-do-it" Hubert reaction, and was enthusiastic instead, he had felt pleasantly tired. "Today my mind just followed my body, no brooding and I started the day slowly." On the couch he allowed thoughts simply to arise and was silent more often. "The couch is helpful. I'm not so reactive anymore. It's about me now, and not what you want. Briefly I thought I should have been able to do this earlier, but I can just *be* now, without pushing myself." Chuckling, I said: "Hard work, huh?"[7] The most difficult issue that prompted his move onto the couch and which he now wanted to tackle was his relationship with women. We had dealt with his burn-out, now we approached his loneliness. He felt that he had put his personal stamp on his work, now he felt sad about all the lost time without a relationship. The word "eunuch" popped into his mind: "One knows how it works, but can't do it. Women always just happened to me. I don't want to go to those 'singles events'. That would be like begging for someone like me, who is used to doing everything on his own. It would be like getting a consolation prize. It lacks dignity. I don't want it to be like an act of desperation. So now I approach the women I know well at the office and ask them to go out. That's not embarrassing anymore. Of course, they're married, but I do realize that I have to show myself. And I found this scientific group of funky, diverse people who discuss the impossibility of alien contact. They're interesting people and I might meet someone, not that there are a lot of women there."

He then remembered his first two relationships in his late teens, which were both loving and intimate, but which he ended abruptly. He makes a point of saying that these relationships and in particular the intimacy occurred at the wish of both participants. He subsequently dreams of these two young women, of being in love with them, but feeling scared and fleeing. In the dream he talked to them, but they left and he looked forlornly after them, felt sad about another missed opportunity, but he thought, it's better this way, it's not for me. I asked him why he felt it's not for him and why he stressed that the initiative for intimacy was equally distributed. He answered by describing a woman at an office party whom he had found extremely attractive and funny, a "whirling dervish", who had shown an obvious interest in him. This had led to a state of over-excitement and paralysis. Following the two youthful loves, he had always split sex and love in his brief affairs. With the "whirling dervish" the fit was too good, that made the stakes too high. "I start to talk myself out of it then. I'd be a cradle robber, she's too young. In my family and in our firm, you didn't show yourself. I would have had to step out the shadows. When I imagine a serious involvement I always get thrown out in the end."

Sex with someone who appealed to him seemed to be the stumbling block. We discussed how he defines himself as a man. It became clear that to directly pursue a woman would have too many connotations of his view of his crude father and, in particular, his father's statements to his sisters when they had boyfriends about the home not being a whorehouse, while at the same time being witness to his father slapping women's bottoms. The "cradle robber" image is connected and in contradiction to a pristine sense of loyalty to his sisters, to whom he ascribes this judgmental imagery of a "cradle robber" about him, should he openly desire and pursue an attractive woman. Being the one to take the initiative would make him into a victimizer and he would feel guilty. Thus he consoles women, and otherwise, he waits. He says the atmosphere at home was "Protestant".

Faced with all this shame and guilt, I answered that it reminded me of a joke in a recently popular Berlin play, where a man goes looking for an ecologically- and politically-correct cooking course. He opens the door to a room and asks whether this is for beginners and gets the answer, "No, this is an advanced course, this is Baking without Flour." So he goes to the next room, where there are 20 men face-down on the floor pumping up and down doing push-ups and asks again what course this is and is answered by "This is Sex without Women." Basically we were now dealing with oedipal issues. The role his mother played was soon to become clearer. In his childhood he had been confronted with a rejecting, belittlingly competitive father and a mother who made sexually-connotated narcissistic use of him, but was otherwise unavailable. His protective stance towards his sisters was due to a generalization of his oedipal feelings for his mother and became crystallized into the roles as consoler for his mother and protector of his sisters in face of the attacks by his father. Thus with women he was locked into a prison of loyalty which inhibited a guilt-free sense of initiative.

The admittedly questionable story in terms of political correctness was a humorous attempt to mirror his predicament.[8] In general, I have found in my work with men of Daniel's generation that the role of the consoler and understander of women is a variation of the oedipal theme in terms of the current Zeitgeist. They are conflicted and insecure about their sense of maleness. To be overtly assertive in their wishes towards women is over-shadowed by the authoritarian and at the same time neglectful images of father that they reject. Lacking a positive male identity, they ultimately feel lost in and engulfed by their relationships with women. "Had I stayed another half year with Katja, I would have been bled out", is the way Daniel put it. In their view of their fathers and men, they feel an accusatory disappointment. In their relationships with women, the archaic ties to mother with the attendant threat of fragmentation, should they dare to loosen those ties by attempting to develop an authentic sense of their male volition also blocks their sense of initiative.

To mention once again our similar life themes: in my childhood I also felt impelled to protect my mother and my younger sister from the attacks of my father. My mother used me as a confidante in terms of her ongoing misery with my father, while she made it clear to me in unmistakable language that in terms of manhood I could never measure up to my brother.

With Daniel I now pointedly focused on the issue of sexuality. I wanted a deeper understanding of his fear of intimacy. He told me that sleeping with a woman, even once, was like signing a contract for life. "In my fantasy I will get the boot sooner or later and then I'm left there like an idiot with my contract in hand. It's a romantic vision that I have. I mean it. I'm not going to go running after the next attractive woman I see. My sense of self-worth is connected to that I won't do that, not that I will!" I answered that there were two sides to the coin: he feels a deep sense of romantic loyalty, but he also feels bled out. "That's why who I choose is so important, but it leaves me paralyzed. I must know that neither of us will use the other."

As stated repeatedly, I have described my life themes, or organizing principles, in order to demonstrate how they influenced the bi-directional level of interaction. As soon as I began to come into contact with Daniel's story, my own became activated; even as I struggled to comprehend Daniel as a distinct person with a unique history, no perception of mine was not co-determined by the images that I held within. This does not mean we are the same. We are different. However, as soon as we began to interact, a new intersubjective field was created in which each of our distinct life-themes became entangled. For instance, I have tried to show how our sense of humor evolved and how this led to transformations in both of us. As I was able to make closer contact with Daniel, I was able to change my needling use of humor into a joyful and pleasurable joint exploration of our relatedness. Thus, in turn, the issue of size took on a new meaning for me. I was released from a sense of awkwardness concerning my big size *vis-à-vis* someone who is smaller in stature, and by extension, the legitimacy of the expression of my expansiveness with others was consolidated. For Daniel, the humor, once he had also overcome its defensive, combative use, allowed pictures of himself to develop, in which showing himself in his own authenticity did not immediately trigger shame and a return to the safety, the isolation, and the loneliness of the shadows. He changed his work habits and put his "personal stamp" on his job.

My own knowledge of my dynamic of self-sacrifice in the service of needed archaic ties, be it with mother or brother, allowed me to resonate deeply with Daniel's fears and the absolute necessity of going through life as a lonesome cowboy. The necessity of my own "response-machine" was one past source for the choice of my profession. While I have transcended this organizing principle through the discipline of many years of practice, the working-through of this psychological phenomenon will never end. Nonetheless the process with Daniel opened up new spaces for reflection in both of us individually, as we used humor as a way to be with one another in such a manner that allowed laughing together about our limitations, which in turn strengthened our bond. Humor threw a wrench in our response-machines and opened a path to authenticity.[9]

In his relationship with his father there has been a role reversal in that his father unburdens himself to Daniel. There is a difference, however, in that Daniel now leaves home without guilt feelings when he wants to and he feels a healthy detachment from his family. Daniel corrects me with enthusiasm and assertively. The parallel working through of my brother transference with his father transference as they became enmeshed allowed us to overcome our penchant for moving in the shadows. The development of the bi-directional process has allowed me a greater freedom in what I can express on the asymmetric level. I think that Daniel's experience of having a male ally that he trusts and the new-found sense of loyalty in his own authentic maleness will facilitate the untying of the paralyzing knot he experiences with women. This remains a work in progress. We shall see how this further changes us and where it takes Daniel.

If the development of humor, as Kohut believes, is the result of our acceptance of our limitations and our transience, then our failures – which in this context are viewed as synonymous with our subjectivity – could be seen in a different light – namely as a bond with our fellow "brothers and sisters in darkness" (Stolorow, 2007). If I look at the structure of Daniel's and my life themes, then I can describe it with the following characteristics: big–small, top–bottom, included–excluded, white sheep–black sheep, present–hidden, expansive–contracted, trusting–afraid. From this I can extrapolate our central issue: a sense of personal annihilation and the highways and by-ways we took to regain a sense of a distinct, agentic selfhood, not only without loss of the bond, but through the medium of the bond. In any psychotherapeutic process the issues that we are dealing with in our respective lives will come together within the intersubjective field and will be worked through on the microscopic level of the bi-directional encounter. This occurs regardless of the difference of levels of structuralization, or any other difference, including the role distribution of therapist and patient. The asymmetric setting defines those roles as well as the purpose and the delimitations of our meeting, such as the length and number of sessions. Furthermore, even as the goal of psychotherapy is the hopefully healing encounter we engage in with the "suffering stranger" (Orange, 2011), on the minute level of mutual influencing, the point will be how we both become strangers no more. This means that it is the totality of each selfhood – and that includes our seeming similarities – that is subjected to an ongoing transformation in the encounter with one another.

My usage of vivid imagery, which included stories that I told about life and which were therefore revealing about myself, and the joint development of humor, led to a twinship experience in which we could share our essential humanity. In Lachmann's words: "through humor and spontaneity we can also achieve an incomparable degree of intimacy that is hard to match through other avenues" (Lachmann, 2003; in: Bodansky, 2004, p. 308).

Notes

1 In emotional dwelling one does not only try to understand the other's experience from their viewpoint, but participates in the other's emotional pain by drawing on analogous experiences of one's own. "Empathic (introspective) understanding is thus grasped as an emergent property of a dialogic system, rather than as a privileged possession of an isolated mind" (Stolorow, 2013).
2 "Developmental trauma originates within a formative intersubjective context whose central feature is malattunement to painful affect, leading to a child's loss of affect-integrating capacity and, thereby, to an unbearable, overwhelmed, disorganized state" (Atwood and Stolorow, 2013).
3 Aron credits Stolorow, Atwood and Ross with introducing the concept of intersubjectivity into psychoanalysis in 1978.
4 "One consequence of developmental trauma, relationally conceived, is that affect states take on enduring, crushing meanings; from recurring experience of malattunement, the child acquires the unconscious conviction that unmet developmental meanings and reactive painful feeling states are manifestations of a loathsome defect or of an inherent inner badness" (Atwood and Stolorow, 2013).
5 "I always felt reassured when I see a glimpse of the capacity for humor, enough security in the self to appreciate the relativity of the self and the recognition of other selves" (Kohut, 1985, p. 239).
6 "Sarcasm occurs in consequence of the lack of idealized values and attempts to minimize the emotional significance of narcissistic limitations through the hyper-cathexis of a pleasure-seeking omnipotent self" (Kohut, 1985, p. 122).
7 "Kohut suggests that humor, as a transformation of narcissism and not merely an expression of denial, can be used in the acceptance of transience. When present, humor contains a sense of quiet inner triumph, mixed with undeniable melancholy that differs from the picture of fragmentary or defensive grandiosity and elation" (Siegel, 1996, p. 62).
8 "When we react not in an analytic manner or too spontaneous we may be apt to criticize ourselves and feel criticized by colleagues. The inner question may arise 'why did I say that?' Thus what may in the short term appear not to be an optimal response may in the long term prove to be more sustaining and human than we realize. In fact it may sometimes be far more beneficial to the patient than our deepest interpretations" (Bodanksy, 2004, p. 306).
9 "In order to to enter with patients and share with them new worlds of experience a use of humor can make the opening of these new doors that much easier for our patients and for us. Let us not neglect a source of strength and cohesion that in different situations can provide needed forms of vitality" (Bodansky, 2004, p. 308).

Chapter 5

Supervision from an intersubjective perspective

I would like to frame my discussion of supervision by two statements made to me by supervisees and two corresponding memories I have of supervision when I was a candidate in psychoanalytic training in the early 1980s in New York. After our hour of supervision one candidate said to me: "I am so glad that I don't feel afraid anymore when I present my therapeutic work to you." To this I responded: "That's the one thing I want to hear as your supervisor." The other supervisee, who is a colleague commented: "For me, what is most important is that supervision is not based on a right-or-wrong attitude, that there is a tolerance for making mistakes and that different perspectives lead to different solutions." I agreed whole-heartedly and had a memory of my own supervision with Crayton Rowe, a self-psychologist. At the time I was at the beginning of my training and presented my material from what he then termed a traditional "drive-defense model". As a novice I was initially somewhat aware of my nervousness about discussing my treatments with a well-seasoned, respected senior supervisor. However, it was the sentence with which he regularly introduced his contributions that only over time made it clear to me just how afraid I had been. He would preface his statements with the words: "I don't want to cut the roast beef too thin, but could we also look at what your patient might be saying like this?" He would then offer me his perspective and we would discuss it. The tentativeness and the kindness with which he framed his supervisory comments allowed me to eventually relax. It also made it clear to me just how vulnerable I had felt and how much he had done to make me feel safe. The other memory I have is of my preparation of a control case for my final presentation as a candidate. I recall telling my control analyst, Joan Klein, how overwhelmed I felt by the telephone book-sized package of notes on my patient that I had to reduce to a 30-minute oral case presentation. She not only helped me to order the mass of raw data of a four-year analytic treatment into a coherent case description, but was instrumental in regulating my fearful affect states. These experiences from my training served as role models for my work as a supervisor.

If one studies the history of the debate in psychoanalysis on how to conduct supervision, one can see how the discussion focuses on the role that the personality of the analyst has in treatment, and how to reconcile a consideration of this with the instructive task of supervision. Initially it was the Hungarian School headed by Michael and Alice Balint – with the influence of Sándor Firenczi hovering in the background – that recognized this as a conundrum and tried to find a solution by incorporating an awareness of the effect of the personality of the therapist on therapy into the process of supervision.[1] While even at this early date psychoanalysts recognized that the personality of the analyst must be understood as an instrument of analysis, the question arose as to what this meant for supervision, a question which is debated until today. The Hungarian School proposed that the first control case of a student analyst be supervised by his or her analyst, arguing that only the analyst could be aware of the role that the personality of the trainee analyst played in the treatment. A debate about supervision ensued which, according to Rosbrow (1997, in Bacal, 2011, p. 128) led to a "teach–treat split as a false dichotomy based on the spurious premise that only interpretive work is legitimate in analysis and only instruction is appropriate in supervision". In 1947, the "London Standing Rules" were proclaimed by the British Psychoanalytic Society prohibiting training analysts from supervising the cases of the student analysts that were in their personal analysis. The International Psychoanalytic Association had, however, already established the "tripartite" system of analytic training since 1925 – the so-called Eitingen model – "with the strict separation of its three modalities: the psychoanalysis of the candidate, the treatment of cases under supervision, and theoretical lectures and seminars" (Bacal, 2011, p. 129). While this agreement constituted a solution on an organizational level, it did not solve the complex demands and seeming paradoxes of the supervisory situation. It did not answer the question whether the supervisee's subjectivity should be addressed as a part of the supervisor's instructive task.

A more process-oriented attempt to resolve the inherent tension between the idiosyncratic impact of the analyst's personality and the

instruction of an analytic theory and technique based on an objecti-
fied epistemology and a standardized application of analytic technique was to circumscribe and delineate the therapist's subjectivity as
counter-transference. Counter-transference was initially conceptualized as pertaining to reactions of the analyst triggered by the patient.
It was viewed as a contaminant of the understanding of transference,
understood as inadequately analyzed aspects of the analyst's personality and as a hindrance for treatment. Later, in a first widening of the
concept, it was seen as an illuminant of the patient's unconscious
(Heimann, 1950). This was a first step in acknowledging a mutual
influence between patient and therapist. While both views of the
counter-transference provided a limited acknowledgment of the role
of the therapist's subjectivity, it simultaneously relegated it outside
the supervisory process by viewing it as a problem that the therapist
was called upon to address through further analysis, or by attributing
it solely to the patient.

We can resolve the dichotomy of teach–treat, instruction–interpretation, objectivity–subjectivity, contaminant–illuminant if we apply
the basic tenets of intersubjectivity theory to the supervisory situation. If supervision is conceptualized as an intersubjective field which
is constituted by the three subjectivities of its participants and if
meaning in human subjectivity is assumed to be context-dependent,
then the dichotomies collapse. The co-constitution of the intersubjective field and the context-dependent interpretation of human meaning
apply both to the context of supervision and treatment. The difference between treatment and supervision becomes clear by examining
the interrelated asymmetric and bidirectional levels of discourse. On
the asymmetric level, the focus of the supervisory work will be on
assisting the supervisee in the understanding, unfolding, illumination
and in the transformation of the subjectivity of the patient. The asymmetric level between supervisor and supervisee pertains to the roles
both participants have in this particular setting and concerns the
goals of supervision. A clinician seeking supervision, and in particular if they are candidates – will be seeking someone whom they regard
as having expertise, knowledge and experience that they do not. Thus
there is a disproportionate amount of power in the setting, which
may be furthered by the fact that the supervisor may be called upon
to evaluate the supervisee. The setting and goal of supervision also
contribute to the asymmetry in that the focus will be on the training
needs of the supervisee – or, of someone seeking expertise – and on
the therapeutic needs of the patient. So while the role distribution

between supervisor and supervisee is a necessary given, the question remains whether the supervisee experiences this as helpful or daunting. At this point my introductory remarks become relevant.

Let us examine the fears expressed by both supervisees in terms of the pathological accommodation to an imagined psychoanalytic or psychotherapeutic ideal, "passed down over a hundred years of traditionalism: we must know, we must predict, we must cure" (Jaenicke, 2014, p. 21) and to the concomitant discussion about success and failure addressed in the first chapter. In its most deleterious form isolated-mind thinking strives for an invulnerable sense of autonomy and mastery on the basis of the belief in a hostile environment and therefore with an understandable defensive predilection for proclaiming universal, objectifiable "truths". If a supervisor's subjectivity is embedded in such an epistemological stance, then he or she will impart to the supervisee that there is a correct way and a wrong way to practice psychotherapy and that he or she will be the judge of whether the supervisee succeeds or fails. At this point, my description may seem like a caricature of some analytic approaches to supervision. Let us see, however, as we deepen our examination of the supervisory process how the source of these fears may be understood in light of the phenomenological contextualism of intersubjectivity theory. We may then be astounded to discover how fear remains a factor for both the practice of supervision and psychotherapy, but that the explanation will be a very different one. If we as supervisors support a view of human nature that can be understood in universally-applicable categories of development and pathology, then it follows that there will be a right or wrong technique applicable to specifically defined diagnostic criteria. The implication for the supervisee is that if he can master this knowledge he will be able to "fix" the patient, and if he does not, he will fail. Both of my supervisees expressed variations of a fear of failure in the eyes of the supervisor who was imagined to have a God's-Eye view of the truth.

If, however, the stance of the supervisor is based on the assumption that meaning in human subjectivity is context-dependent, then everything that emerges from the field can only be understood through an examination of the various forms of mutual influencing occurring between the three protagonists co-constituting the field. Therefore the candidates' fears in an intersubjectively-informed supervision will not revolve around whether what they are doing is wrong or right in terms of "fixed frames of reference, such as specific developmental stages or defensive maneuvers" (Buirski and Haglund, 2001, p. 176)[2] but rather whether they are able to enter into a dialogue in which they are asked to understand the patient's unique subjective experience in which they themselves have a constitutive role. Once the supervisee begins to grasp the far-reaching ramifications of being implicated in everything the patient does and the context-dependent nature of all meaning of subjective experience, and that this contextualist perspective applies both to training and treatment, he or she may feel overwhelmed. No longer being able to rely on an objectivist theory about human development and pathology does not lead so much to a fear of being wrong, but to a fear of the consequences of the imperfections of their own subjectivity. If the supervisor is, however, able to impart a clinical sensibility which is based on an understanding that any interaction of differently organized subjective worlds in psychotherapy will show how closely weakness and strength are entwined, how both the emotional worlds of the patient and the analyst play a constitutive role, as do the successes and failure of any therapeutic process, then the interaction of the supervisory dyad can become a model for the therapeutic dialogue between the supervisee and his patient. The supervisor can, as I have outlined in the first chapter, convey to the supervisee that rather than bracketing his or her subjectivity, the idiosyncratic strengths and short-comings of both participants will become entangled on the bidirectional level as a matter of course and can then be subsequently dealt with in the working-through process.

We can resolve the seeming dichotomies and paradoxes of supervision mentioned earlier (teach–treat; instruction–interpretatiom; objectivity–subjectivity; contaminant–illuminant) if we understand them instead in terms of the relationship between the asymmetric and the bi-directional levels of discourse. In this view, the asymmetric role of the supervisor is embedded in and seen as a product of his or her awareness of the level of mutual influencing between the three participants. The perspectives that we offer as supervisors will be given as a reflection of our limited *subjective understanding* of our experience of a once-removed patient. It will attempt to include an understanding of the impact that the supervisee has on the patient and on us, as well as a consideration of the effect we have on the supervisee. This means that whatever we offer will be imparted in a tentative spirit based on our awareness of the complexities of simultaneously being an actor in and a product of an intersubjective field.

Does this appreciation of the complexity of the field infer that we hide our expertise, that we do not attempt to guide our supervisees and to differentiate between more or less helpful interventions? No, it does not; but it does have a significant impact on how we understand our task and which methods we use to implement it. On the bi-directional level of discourse, the goal of supervision, in my view, is to help the supervisee practice our profession in a manner that suits his or her personhood and allows an unfolding and creative use of who they are, and who they are not, in the particularity of the interchange with each unique patient and the demands of each specific field. The challenge for the supervisor is to enter into a dialogue with the supervisee which will entail working through the similarities and differences of perspective. This encounter of the differently organized subjective worlds of the supervisor and supervisee is the essence of working on the bi-directional level in which anything and everything about the supervisor and everything and anything about the supervisee will impact upon one another and on the task at hand. While my focus and responsibility are on the supervisee and the patient, a great part of my personal incentive and satisfaction in being a supervisor derives from being allowed to take part in the unpredictable development of the supervisee in his or her distinctness as a therapist. I stress the unpredictability of the process of supervision in order to emphasize two interrelated points: that we cannot know beforehand how our subjective world will interact and impact the supervisee and that it is precisely the uncertainties of this challenge that provide supervisors with the opportunity to enhance their skills.

In a recent study spanning 15 years of research by John Hattie (2008) about what enables students to learn, it wasn't the specific teaching methods, but the believability of the teacher, the ability to see the subject matter from the point of view of the student, to give individual feedback to each particular student, to question oneself and to teach in a dialogical manner. From an intersubjective point of view, the teacher teaches the student, but the student makes the teacher a teacher.

After having attempted to illuminate the theoretical premises of supervision from an intersubjective perspective, I would now like to turn to a more practical enumeration of the tasks of supervision based on my own experience.

1. The first task is to create an atmosphere of safety for the supervisee. Understanding that in our profession we are our own

instruments necessitates a constant awareness of the vulnerability inherent in discussing our work. In working with candidates this means being conscious of the intimate and personal and potentially explosive nature of our work, the possibly confusing heterogeneity of the theories, and the difference of approaches of the supervisors they will be confronted with. In other words, an awareness on the part of the supervisor of how overwhelming it can be to be in training and how long it may take to even begin to get one's bearings.

2. Getting to know the idiosyncratic personality of the supervisee and how this is expressed in his or her therapeutic work is another essential. This entails a dialogic form of discussion with many questions why a supervisee said or did what they did, as well as questions about what they wanted to say, but didn't. It includes offering my own perspective, with an attitude to select and use what feels right for them and to throw the rest overboard. The task is to convey the idea that there is no one right way of being a therapist or analyst, but rather to constantly monitor how patients assimilate our personalities and the entire relationship with us into their experiential worlds.

3. To convey an attitude of fallibility concerning our own subjective understanding: that we don't understand at least as much as that we do understand and that while we strive to do our best, imperfection is a constant companion. Facing the enormous complexity and weight of responsibility of psychotherapy is easier to bear when we can treat insecurity as an asset, rather than an enemy. The intersubjective motto is: "it depends".

4. While we are aware of the fact that the focus of psychoanalysis is on the intersection of therapist and patient, and that in supervision that co-constitution of the field includes the supervisor, our task is not the analysis of the supervisee. If, however, blockages in the psychotherapeutic process due to either a too great similarity or dissimilarity in the experiential worlds of supervisees and their patients occur, then the supervisor may choose to carefully address how the supervisee's subjectivity may be impacting the treatment. This is done within the circumscribed context of the clinical exchange with the primary purpose of facilitating the treatment of the patient. The first task of the supervisor will be to validate and contain the affect of the supervisee. Frequently this will pertain to the subjective danger the supervisee experiences as his or her experiential worlds become challenged by their

patients. It may suffice for the supervisor to point out the general problematic area of the supervisee, and to advise working through this issue, either by themselves or with their training analysts. In some instances, a limited, circumscribed discussion of the doubts and fears that are blocking the supervisee's ability to decenter and re-open the empathic channel to his or her patient may be called for, however, only to the degree that both supervisee and supervisor are comfortable with. The primary purpose here is not to re-create a teach–treat split, but rather to enhance the *awareness* of the supervisee of the impact of his or her subjectivity. As stated earlier, this awareness of the bi-directional nature of human interchange also includes the impact that supervisor and supervisee have on one another. The purpose of self-reflection in supervision is in the service of dealing with difficulties in the supervisee's therapeutic task and is not intended to replace his or her own psychotherapy. Particularly in instances where enactments occur, an intersubjective approach is invaluable, because enactments, just like everything occurring in the field, are a product of the field. When dissociated states in the patient meet dissociated states in the supervisee, enactments may be the result. In this case, it may be the task of the supervisee to first become aware of how his pre-reflective, or dynamically repressed unconscious, or dissociated states are instrumental in the patient's increasing concretizations. The supervisee's self-reflection may then suffice to interrupt a blockage that, if left unattended, could lead to an interruption or termination of treatment.

5. In summary, the clinical attitude with which I attempt to approach my supervisees is what Orange (2011) has conceptualized as a hermeneutics of trust. It is a variation of my credo: "believe your patients", in that it is the supervisor's task to help the supervisee attain the trust that is necessary to express what they feel about their patients and how they understand them. "Trust yourself" is the message that I repeatedly give to my supervisees. This includes trying things out with patients and that making mistakes is a part of our work, which can always be mitigated if we continually monitor the effect of our interventions on our patients. Perhaps seemingly paradoxical, I also try to convey the centrality of a corner-stone of psychoanalysis: the unconscious. Jokingly I remark that: "They don't call it unconscious for nothing!" Actually, it is not so easy to convey the mighty power of the

unconscious. It can sometimes be quite readily grasped, for instance, in certain kinds of dreams in which the condensed versions of our personal narratives are instantly enlightening. At other times, the difference between how we consciously experience ourselves and what may surface from the unconscious can be so disparate as to be experienced as a blow to the solar plexus, or, at the least, to take our breath away. The difficulty in grasping the unconscious has not changed since Freud's seminal discovery. Perhaps only insofar as we may not attribute the fear of the unconscious so much to a lack of control, as to a felt sense of the vulnerability that our unbearable embeddedness in being entails. The clinical sensibility of fallibilism and of dialogic questioning, the process-oriented mode of understanding, the necessity to leave Gestalts open, the impact of the limitations of our subjectivity, and the imponderabilities of the intersubjective field and of implicit relational knowing are all in part related to the power of the unconscious. Intangibles are part of our profession. The hermeneutics of trust can serve as their holding environment.

6. Empathy, or the ability to listen to our patients is the central method that I try to teach. The use of verbatim protocols is invaluable to this endeavor. Protocols give us the experience-near opportunity to see how and whether the supervisee is tracking the patient's material. Do the interventions further or hinder the unfolding of the patient's subjective world? We can see by the patient's reactions whether the interventions have sidetracked the patient, elicited accommodation, or defensiveness. It also becomes clear whether the patient is able to ignore a supervisee's malattunement and maintain the perception of his or her own experience. If the patient feels understood, it will lead to a deepening of inner experience. Another indicator of our ability to listen is whether the patient's *reaction* to the supervisee–therapist intervention has deepened *his* or *her experience* of the therapeutic relatedness. While I prefer the use of verbatim protocols, I do not insist upon them. Supervisory hours may also be used to address any question the supervisee may have concerning our work, including discussions of theory. I do try to convey the importance of reading texts, offering recommendations while encouraging the supervisee to read according to where his or her interest takes them, including reading only parts of books, or disregarding literature that does not speak to them momentarily.

7. A common mistake that all therapists may succumb to is to disregard the emotional forest and to focus on the content trees. Therefore as a general guideline I recommend searching for the main affect and the unconscious organizing principles underlying what the patient conveys, verbally or non-verbally. Emotions, or affects are what allows us humans to know who we are. "Affect – that is, subjective emotional experience – is something that from birth onward is co-constituted within ongoing relational systems. Emotional experience is inseparable from the intersubjective contexts of attunement and malattunement in which it is felt. Therefore, locating affect at its motivational center automatically entails a radical contextualization of virtually all aspects of human psychological life" (Stolorow, 2013, p. 383). The use of protocols facilitates staying focused on experience-near data and discourages getting lost in all too hypothetical conjectures about the patient.; The unconscious organizing principles refer to those emotional conclusions a patient has unconsciously surmised through the repetitive interactions with his emotional surround about the nature of him- or herself, the other, and the world. These unconscious principles are the building blocks, and in their sum, form the personality of the patient. What are the convictions that patients have drawn about themselves and the nature of life, on the basis of their experiences of mother, father, siblings, and other significant others as well as the cultural surround they were born into?

8. The unconscious conclusions will be directed at the supervisee in the form of the transference. Transference is understood as an organizing activity in which patients assimilate the analytic relationship into their archaic subjective worlds of selfhood and other. Transference is seen as a continuum, on which the patient is either moving towards or away from the supervisee. The continuum is delimited by two poles. On the one end there are all those activities which are organized around growth potentials, which were derailed and seek renewed development in the therapeutic relationship. The other pole is characterized by those affects that expect re-traumatization, that are therefore conflictual and are defensively warded off. The question for the supervisee is, where is the patient on this continuum? The other question is what has the supervisee contributed directly to calling either one or the other form of transference forth, or indirectly

what has the supervisee contributed that has lent itself to being organized in such a manner by the patient? Corresponding to the two dimensions of the transference are the leading- and trailing-edge interpretations: those that correspond to the expansive and those that deal with the conflictual, resistant, re-traumatized elements of the patient's material.

9. Dreams are the microscopic symbolizations of the patient's subjectivity. Supervisees are asked to differentiate between those dreams that serve a cohesion-maintaining function and whose latent content is therefore not in the foreground, and those dreams in which a further decoding of the latent content would be helpful. In the former it is the cohesion-maintaining function that is interpreted. In the latter the latent content is dealt with in the usual manner of allowing the patient to associate to the various elements of the dream and ascertaining its possible message in terms of the intersubjective field, that is the interplay of the two transferences of patient and supervisee. With both forms of dreams, the patient is asked first about the meaning and the central affect.

10. Lastly a discussion of the setting between supervisee and supervisor and supervisee and patient is an important aspect of supervision. Therapeutic and supervisory settings are as varied as there are therapists and supervisors. My own guideline is to offer conditions that make the work possible for me, with supervisees and patients alike. I think that it is important that supervisees offer some kind of structure for themselves and their patients. Structure protects both participants and imparts a sense of continuity and safety, as well as showing that we take the work and our time seriously. As supervisor I attempt to help my supervisees find a structure that they feel comfortable with and feel they can uphold. For all participants the structure of psychotherapy and supervision must take into consideration the specificity of the unique intersubjective field in which it takes place. Every point that I have schematically outlined here is therefore subject to an evaluation as to its applicability within each unique triad or dyad: it depends.

Notes

1 I am grateful to Howard Bacal (2011) for his detailed historical description of the early debates in psychoanalysis concerning supervision and in agreement with the systemic perspective of his specificity theory about the process of supervision.
2 I am indebted to Buirski and Haglund's (2001) excellent chapter on an intersubjective understanding of supervision.

Chapter 6

Epilogue

I consider this book as the third in a psychoanalytic trilogy, that is to say that there has been a development of my thinking which has, I hope, become clearer as it has unfolded. The synonyms for the term epilogue are afterword, and coda. Before tracing the development of what I believe to be the conclusions I have come to so far, I would therefore like to make some general remarks. Throughout my books I have emphasized my limitations, shortcomings and failures in order to make it unequivocally clear that we influence each therapeutic process with every fiber of our personalities. Any therapist's difficulties as a human being may be brought forth as a matter of course by entering into the realms of emotional distress and destruction of their patients.

Taking part in the understanding, illumination and transformation of the experiential worlds of our patients is not an experience that leaves us unscathed, as we have all had our history of suffering. I have attempted to show how shared suffering can be one path that transformation can take. At the same time, I have been at pains to point out that our strengths also play a major part in what occurs in psychotherapy, and that the search for meaning may be as rewarding for therapists as it is for patients. However, because of the uniqueness of each intersubjective field co-constructed by patient and therapist, we cannot know when and how our strengths and weaknesses will affect the therapeutic process. All we can know is that we are always in the thick of it, whether we are bored, distressed, delighted, or whether we feel deeply engaged or detached during the therapeutic processes that we take part in. Throughout my books I have attempted to *show* what the effects were of the highly specific encounters between me and my patients. Whatever happens between us and patients is an unpredictable process which unfolds over time, a process which we as therapists lead and which simultaneously leads us.

I have tried to demonstrate the inter-play between these two levels of discourse, the asymmetric where we lead, and the bi-directional in which we are an ongoing part of a co-construction which we cannot determine beforehand, for which we are, however, responsible. It bears repetition that the unpredictability of therapeutic processes is due to the fluid and dynamic nature of the unconscious, as well as to the uniqueness of the interplay of mutual influencing within any given intersubjective field. As a profession we have been somewhat reluctant to own up to the truism that to change, you have to let yourself be changed. Transformation always involves both partici-pants. It is not only the patient who is called upon to change. Transformation also occurs as a result of the therapist's willingness to shed his psychological skin, to leave his doubts and resistances behind and to completely be on the patient's side. At such moments both participants come together and the process moves. While con-frontation has its legitimate place, finding communality is often the greater challenge. The therapist's ability to maintain a dialogue about the differently organized subjectivities frequently demands a decenter-ing from his or her own experiential world and is thus a part of the transformation a therapist undergoes. The rewards of this task lie in the finding of a co-constructed relational home. We do not heal our patients, rather we are part of a process that is emotionally helpful for both of us, or not. Psychotherapy is such an exceptional and complex undertaking because even as we lead the process in terms of our training and expertise, our therapeutic experience and responsi-bility, as well as by virtue of the fact that the goal is defined by helping our patients, we ourselves co-create and are a part of an on-going, unpredictable interchange. It is as if we are traveling along a road which we jointly pave at each step of the way. In the first book, *The Risk of Relatedness* (2008), I described five central psychoanalytic concepts from an intersubjective perspective: neutrality and its alter-native the empathic-introspective mode of inquiry, affectivity and the paradigm shift in psychoanalysis, trauma, and transference. The dif-ferences between the traditional psychoanalytic conceptualizations and an intersubjective perspective were described through the prism of the risk of relatedness entailed in human encounters in general; and in particular in therapeutic encounters. The emphasis on the risk involved was a first step in my examination of the co-construction of the therapeutic exchange and an initial attempt to shed light on the influence of the bi-directional level of discourse on therapeutic action. In the second book, *Change in Psychoanalysis* (2011), I examined the clinical exchange from the perspective of the three variables that I found to be salient in therapeutic change: the primacy of subjectivity, the primacy of mutual influencing, and the co-determined nature of change. By deepening the description of my own involvement and input into the intersubjective field, I wanted to encourage psychotherapists to lift the *cordon sanitaire* that I felt was obscuring the participation of the therapist's subjectivity in the therapeutic process and thus to enhance the possibility of case descriptions of the intersubjective field in its entirety.

In this, the third book, I further attempted to refine the perspective from which I examined therapeutic action to a study of the interplay between the asymmetric and the bi-directional levels of discourse in the intersubjective field and how this effects therapeutic change. On the asymmetric level we practice psychotherapy with the well-known tools of understanding and illuminating the patient's inner world. We do this by an on-going tracking and naming of the patient's affective states and unconscious organizing principles. This in itself is an arduous and demanding task, requiring discipline and humility. The affect regulation of deep feelings of any nature: be they sorrowful, joyful, or seemingly absent, can be said to be the heart of the psycho-therapeutic endeavor. Emotion is the chief guideline to know who we are. The ability to name, or interpret, the patient's affects and organizing principles is a product of the therapist–patient relation-ship. As the patient's emotional experience becomes increasingly nameable within the context of our understanding, it will become a part of the fabric of who the patient essentially is and enhance his or her sense of being. This, in turn, is the heart of therapeutic change (Stolorow, 2013). The asymmetric level of discourse is not separate from the bi-directional level; it is a part of it. Asymmetric actions can be said to arise out of the bi-directional experience of mutual influ-encing. In my work I have tried to emphasize that therapeutic action is a product of the highly idiosyncratic, and personal inter-mingling of the experiential worlds of the patient and the therapist. In hind-sight, I can now recognize that the developmental line of the three books lies in my wish to describe therapeutic action as precisely as possible from the perspective of phenomenological contextualism. Phenomenological in the exactness with which I was able to describe the worlds of emotional experience, and contextual in terms of how well I was able to demonstrate how emotional experience takes form "both developmentally and in the psychoanalyic situation, in constitutive intersubjective contexts" (p. 383). While the goal of psychotherapy remains the possibility of helping the patient to arrive at his or her own experiential authenticity, or at least to lessen the amount of suffering, both will depend on the degree to which we are successful in sharing a relational home with our patients.

References

Adam-Lauterbach, D. (2013). *Geschwisterbeziehung und seelische Erkrankung*. Stuttgart: Klett-Cotta.

Atwood, G.E. (2012). *The Abyss of Madness*. New York (Routledge).

Atwood, G.E. (2013). http://www.psychologytoday.com/blog/strange-memories/201302/letter-young-student-part-4

Atwood, G.E., and Stolorow, R.D. (1979). *Faces in a cloud: Subjectivity in personality theory*. New York (Jason Aronson).

Atwood, G.E., and Stolorow, R.D. (1984). *Structures of Subjectivity: Explorations in Psychoanalytic Phenomenology*. Hillsdale, NJ (The Analytic Press).

Atwood, G.E., and Stolorow, R.D. (2013). Legacies of the Golden Age: A Memoir of Collaboration. *The Humanistic Psychologist*, 41:285–300.

Bacal, H., and Carlton, L. (2011). *The Power of Specificity in Psychotherapy: When Therapy Works – And When It Doesn't*. New York (Jason Aronson).

Balint, M. (1970). *Regression. Therapeutische Aspekte der Regression. Die Theorie der Grundstörung*. Trans. by K. Hügel. Stuttgart (Klett-Cotta).

Balint, M. (1979). *The Basic Fault*. New York (Brunner/Mazel).

Beebe, B., and Lachmann, F.M. (2002). *Infant Research and Adult Treatment: Co-constructing interactions*. Hillsdale, NJ (Analytic Press).

Bodansky, R. (2004). The Benefit of Humor in Psychoanalysis. *Self Psychology: European Journal for Psychoanalytic Therapy and Research*, 17/18:298–309.

Boston Change Process Study Group (2010). *Change in Psychotherapy: A Unifying Paradigm*. New York (W.W. Norton and Company).

Boston Change Process Study Group (2012). *Veränderungsprozesse. Ein integratives Paradigma*. Übers. von E. Vorspohl. Frankfurt am Main (Brandes & Apsel).

Brandchaft, B., Doctors, S., and Sorter, D. (2010). *Toward an Emancipatory Psychoanalysis: Brandchaft's Intersubjective Vision*. New York (Routledge).

Buirski, P., and Haglund, P. (2001). *Making Sense Together: The Intersubjective Approach to Psychotherapy*. New York (Jason Aronson).

Coburn, W.J. (2007). Psychoanalytic complexity: pouring new wine directly in one's mouth. In: *New Developments in Self Psychology Practice*, Eds. D.P. Buirski and A. Kottler. Northvale, NJ (Aronson).

Coburn, W.J. (2009). Attitudes in psychoanalytic complexity: an alternative to postmodernism in psychoanalysis. In: *Beyond Postmodernism: New Dimensions in Clinical Theory and Practice*, Eds. R. Frie and D. Orange. New York (Routledge).

Das Neue Testament (1968). 1 Corinthians 10,12. Kleinostheim: Paul Pottlach Verlag.

Dylan, Bob (1967). 'Chimes of Freedom', on *Another Side of Bob Dylan* (CD). New York: Sony Music Entertainment, Inc.

Fuqua, P.B. (1999). *Termination: A Conceptual History and a Contemprorary View*. Lecture: The 22nd Annual International Conference on the Psychology of the Self, Toronto.

Goldberg, A. (2012). *The Analysis of Failure: An Investigation of Failed Cases in Psychoanalysis and Psychotherapy*. New York (Routledge).

Hattie, J. (2011). *Visible Learning for Teachers: Maximizing Impact on Learning*. New York (Routledge).

Heisterkamp,G. (2001). Is psychoanalysis a cheerless (Freud-less) profession? Toward a psychoanalysis of joy. *Psychoanalysis Quarterly*, LXX:839–70.

Hoffmann, M.T. (2011). *Toward Mutual Recognition: Relational Psychoanalysis and the Christian Narrative*. New York (Routledge).

Jaenicke, C. (2006a). Die Beendigung von Psychoanalysen. Eine selbst-psychologisch-intersubjektive Sicht, pp.81–92. In: *Die Beendigung von Psychoanalysen und Psychotherapien. Die Achillesferse der psychoanalytischen behandlungstechnik?*, edited by P. Diederichs. Gießen: Psychosozial-Verlag.

Jaenicke, C. (2008). *The Risk of Relatedness. Intersubjectivity Theory in Clinical Practice*. New York (Aronson).

Jaenicke, C. (2011). *Change in Psychoanalysis. An Analyst's Reflections on the Therapeutic Relationship*. New York (Routledge).

Kohut, H. (1966). Forms and transformations of narcissism. *Journal of the American Psychoanalytic Association*, 14:243–72.

Kohut, H. (1985). *Self Psychology and the Humanities: Reflections on a New Psychoanalytic Approach*, Ed. C. Strozier. New York (Norton).

Lachmann, F.M. (2003). *Humor, Spontaneity and Communication in the Therapeutic Process*. Lecture, Rome. In Bodansky, R. (2004), The benefit of humor in psychoanalysis. *Self Psychology. European Journal for Psychoanalytic Therapy and Research*, 17/18:298–309.

Lichtenberg, J.D., Lachmann, F.M., and Fosshage, J.L. (2011). *Psychoanalysis and Motivational Systems: A New Look*. New York (Routledge).

Orange, D.M. (1995). *Emotional Understanding: Studies in Psychoanalytic Epistomology*. New York (The Guilford Press).

Orange, D.M. (2009). Toward the art of the living dialogue: between constructivism and hermeneutics in psychoanalytic thinking. In: *Beyond Postmodernism: New Dimensions in Clinical Theory and Practice*. Eds. R. Frie and D. Orange, New York (Routledge).

Orange, D.M. (2011). *The Suffering Stranger: Hermeneutics for Everyday Clinical Practice*. New York (Routledge).

Pink Floyd (2011 remastered). Another Brick in the Wall. *The Wall* (CD). Parlophone Records Ltd.

Safran, J., and Proskurov, B. (2008). Alliance, negotiation, and rapture resolution. In Lvey, R., and Ablon, J. (Eds), *Handbook of Evidence-based Psychodynamic Psychotherapy* (pp. 201–25). New York (Humana Press/Springer).

Scialfa, Patti (1993). Valerie: *Rumble Doll* (CD). New York (Sony Music Entertainment, Inc).

Scorsese, M. (2007). *Shine a Light*. Paramount Pictures.

Siegel, A.M. (1996). *Heinz Kohut and the Psychology of the Self*. New York (Routledge).

Stern, D. (2012). Lecture. SGAPS-Annual Conference. Brunnen, Switzerland.

Stolorow, R.D. (1997). Dynamic, dyadic, intersubjective systems: An evolving paradigm for psychoanalysis. *Psychanalytic Psychology* 14:337–64.

Stolorow, R.D. (2011). *World, Affectivity, Trauma: Heidegger and Post-Cartesian Psychoanalysis*. New York (Routledge).

Stolorow, R.D. (2013). Intersubjective-Systems Theory: A phenomenological-contextualist psychoanalytic perspective. *Psychoanalytic Dialogues*, 23:383–9.

Thelen, E., and Smith, L. (1994). *A Dynamic Systems Approach to the Development of Cognition and Action*. Cambridge MA (The MIT Press).

Winnicott, D.W. (1965). *The Maturational Processes and the Facilitating Environment*. New York (International Universities Press).

Winnicott, D.W. (1984). *Reifungsprozesse und fördernde Umwelt*. Übers. von G. Theusner-Stampa. Frankfurt am Main (Fischer).

Index

16919950R10066

Printed in Poland
by Amazon Fulfillment
Poland Sp. z o.o., Wrocław